COLORING BOOK VEHICLES FOR TODDLERS

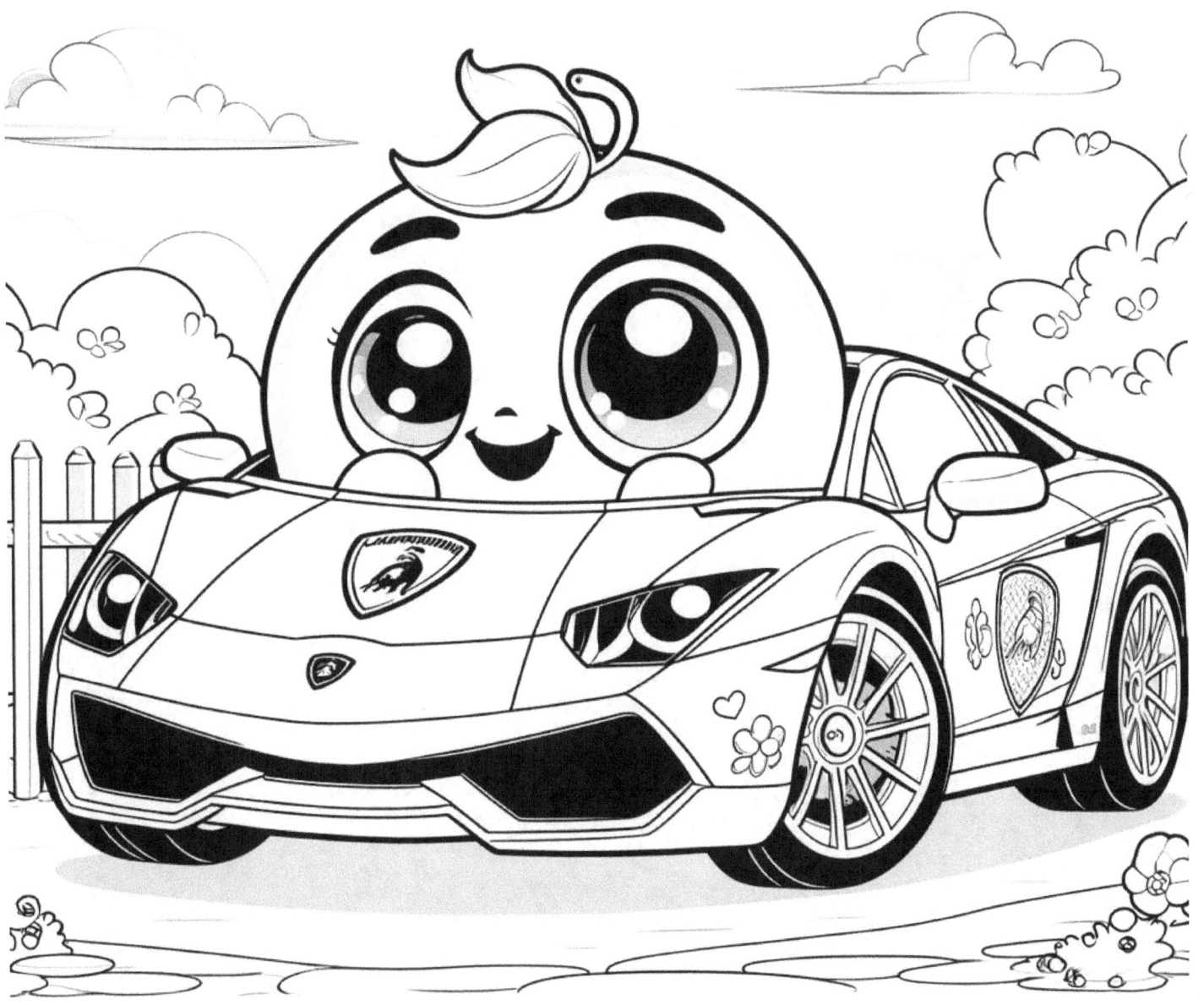

For ages 3 -18

Pérez Arboleda

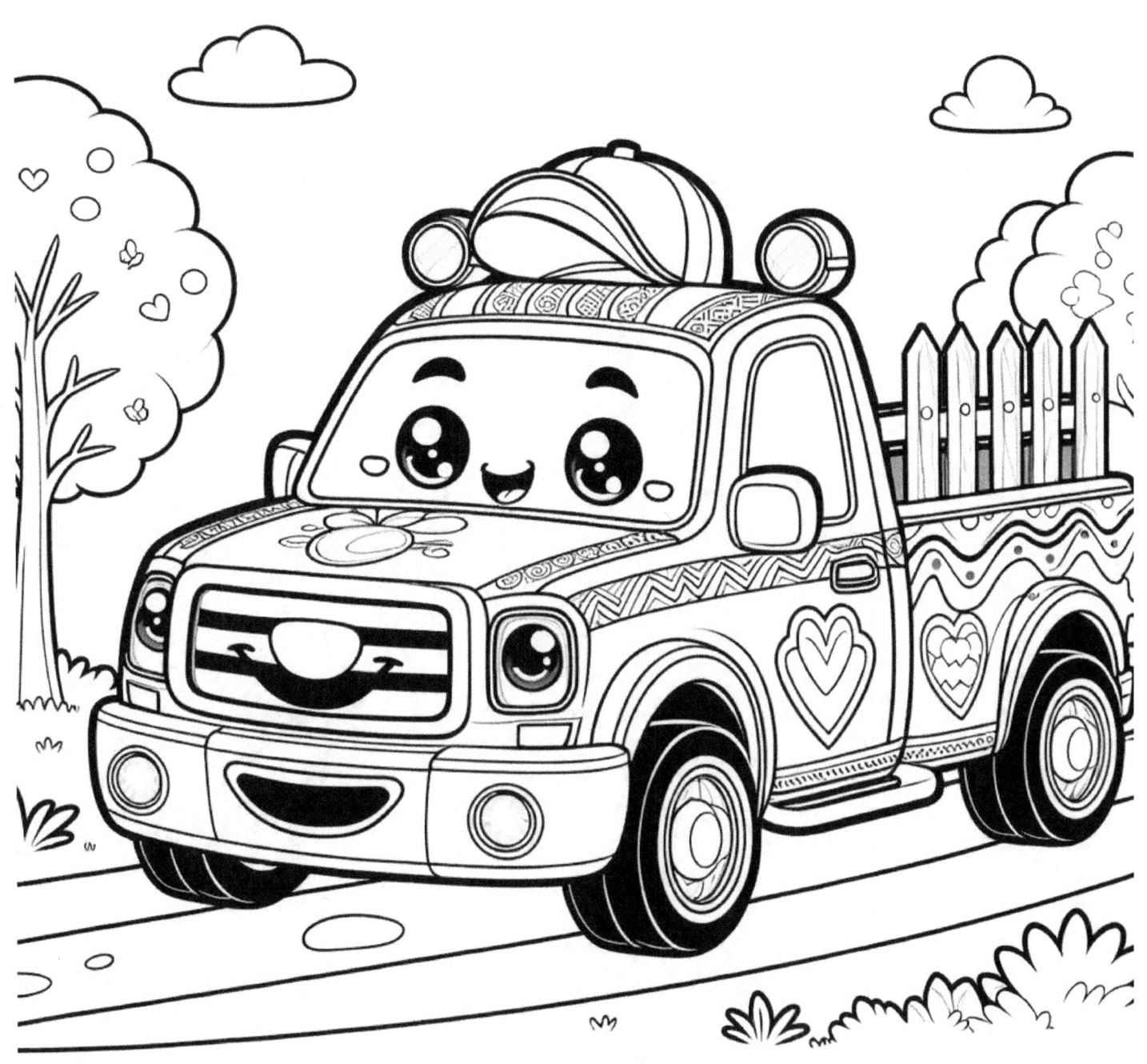

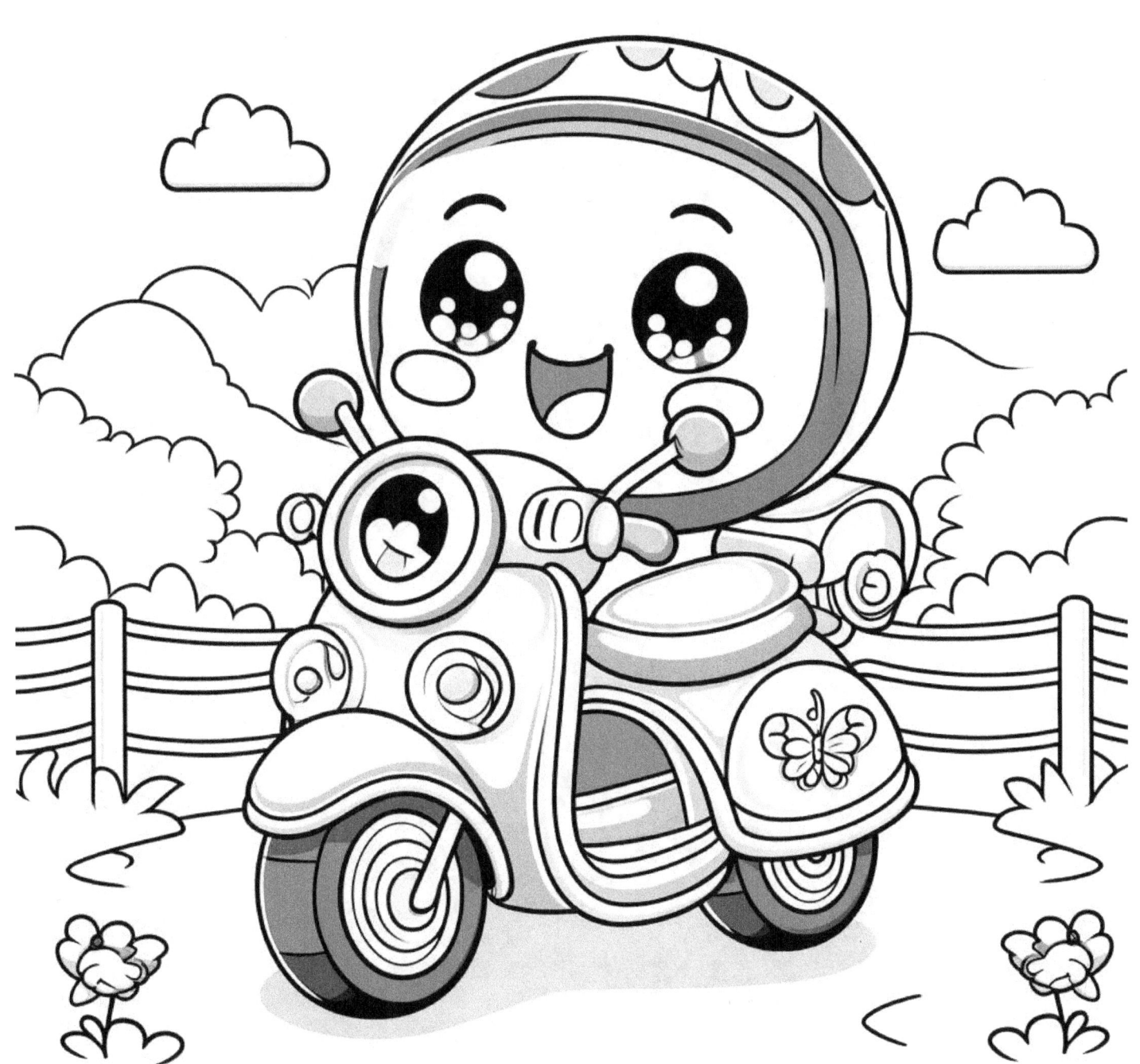

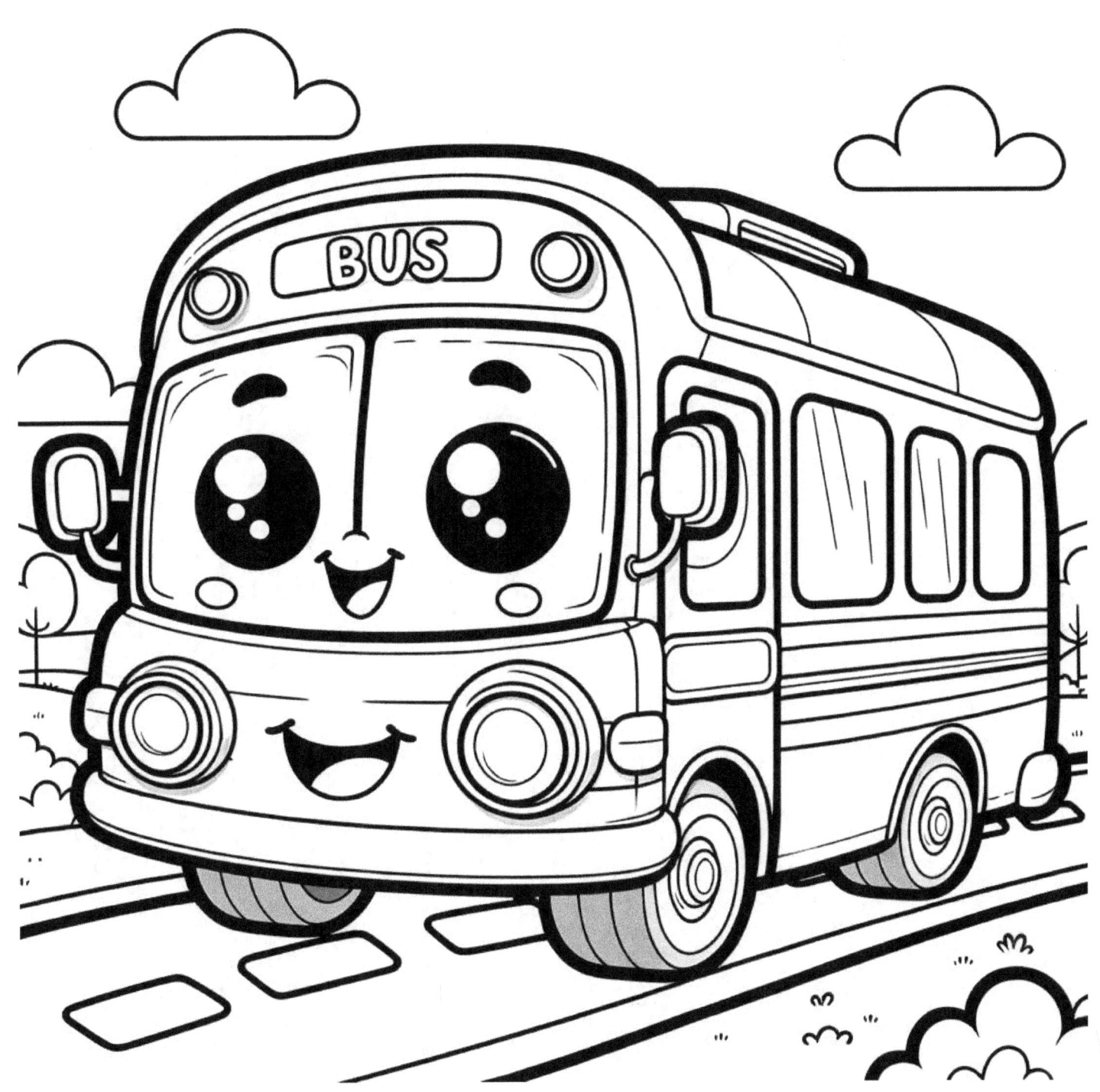

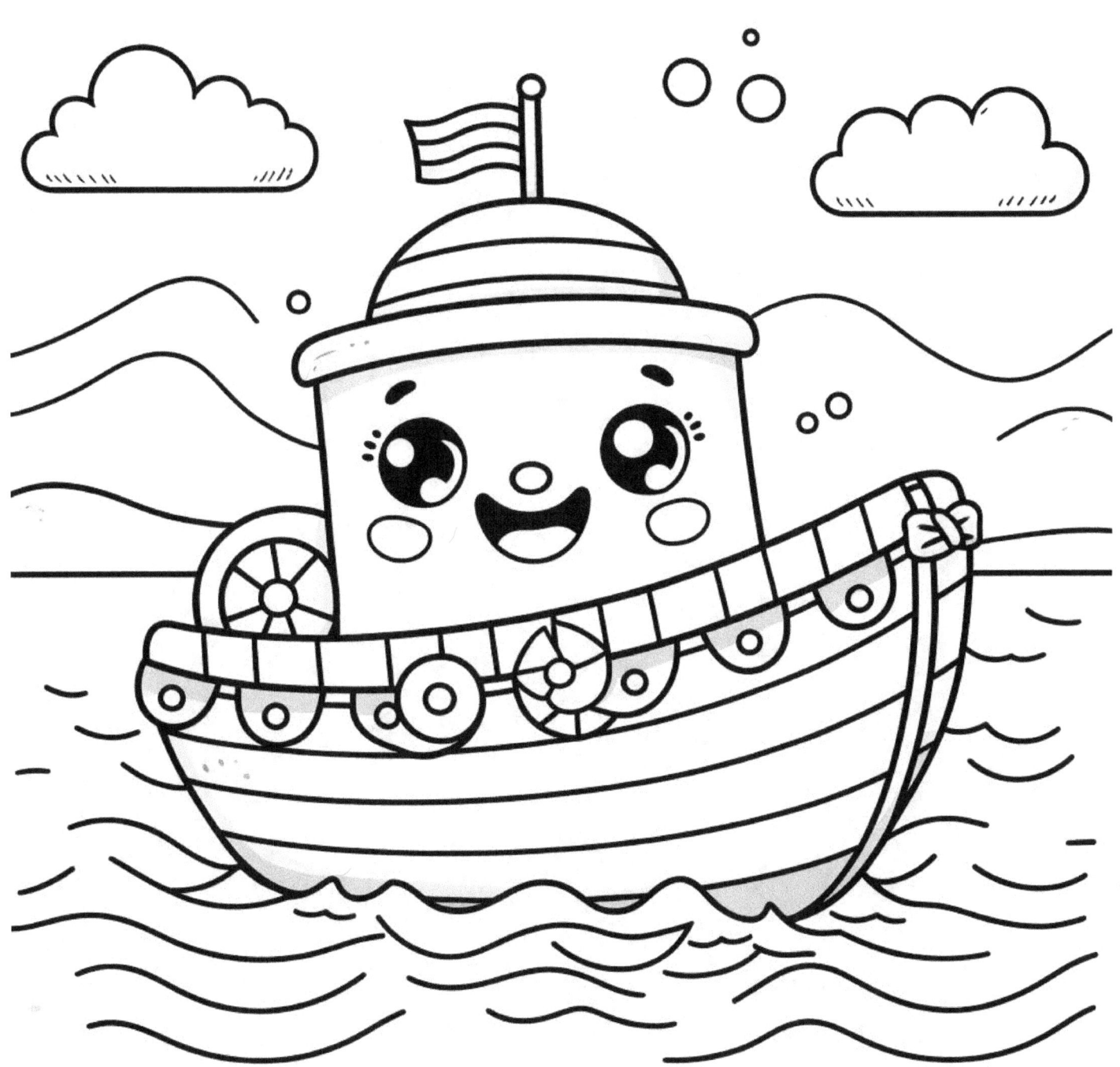

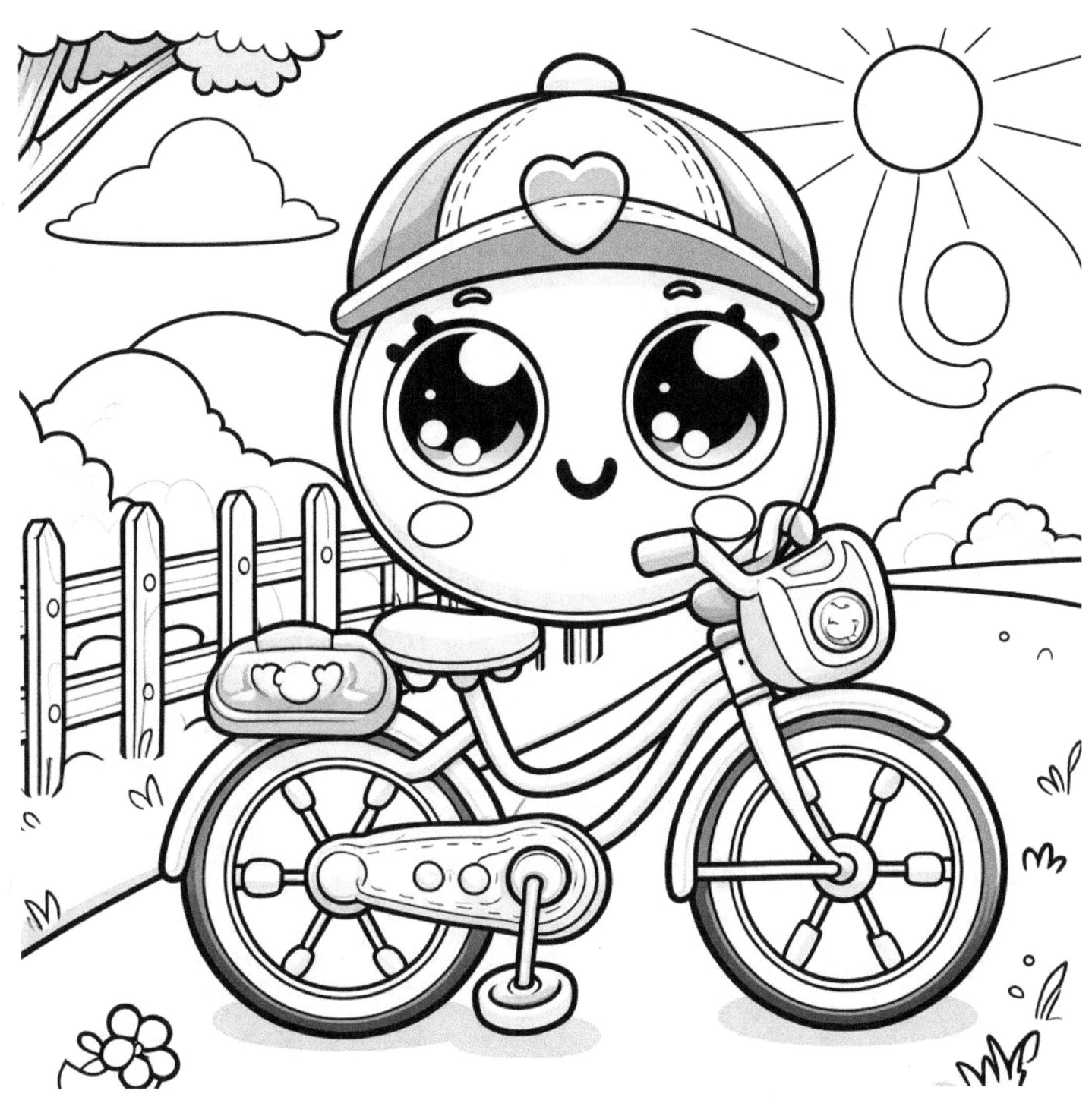

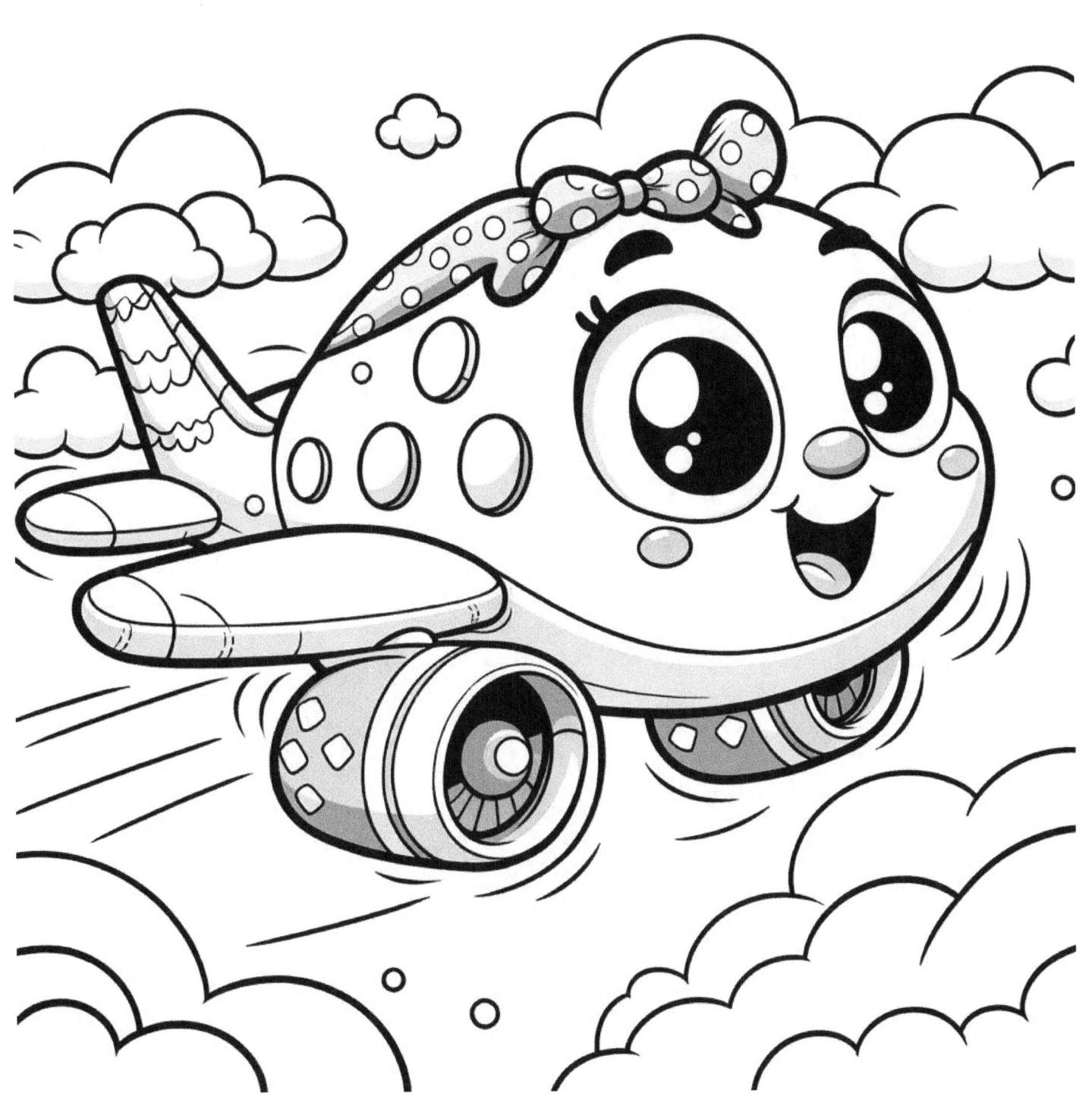

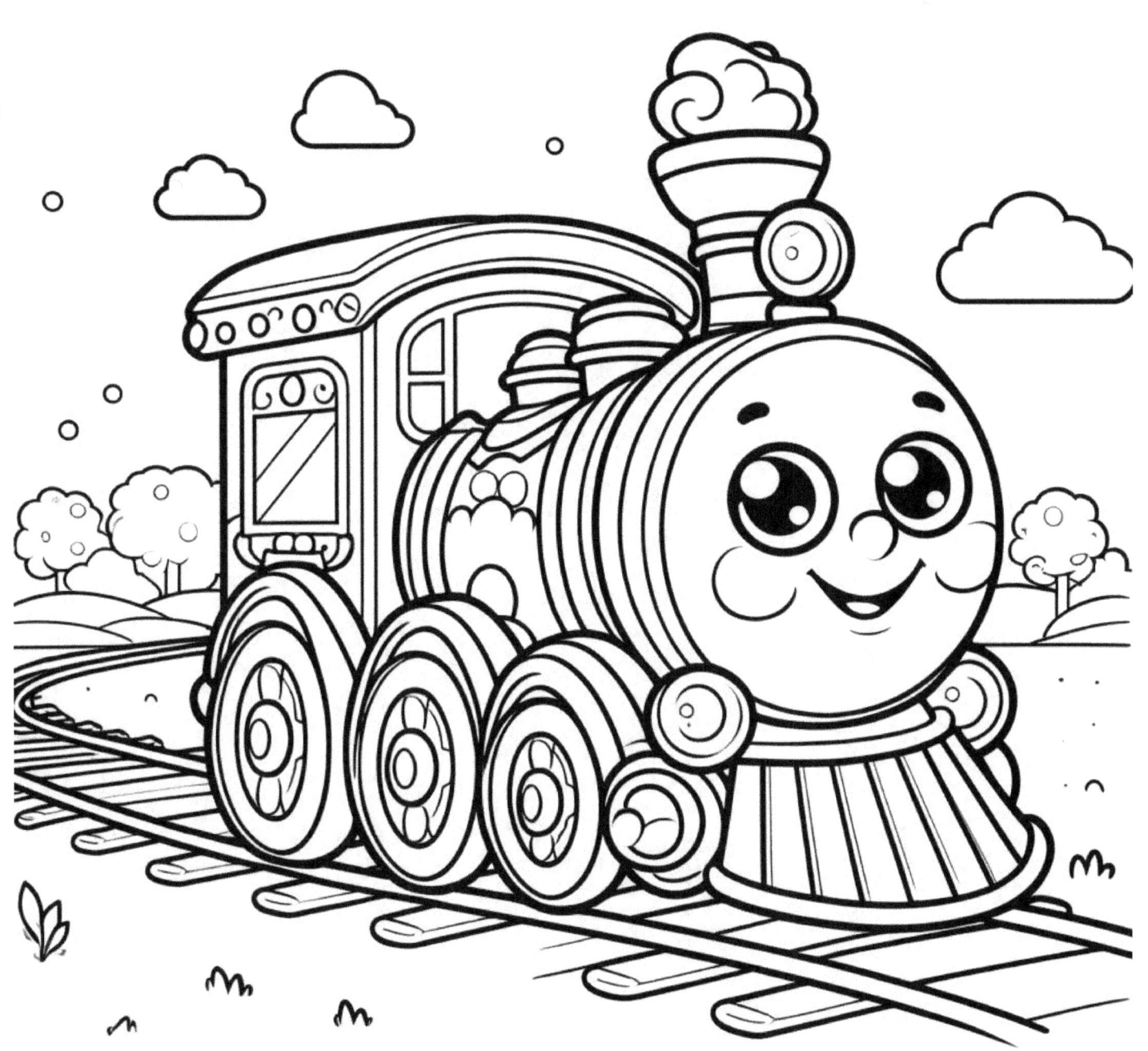

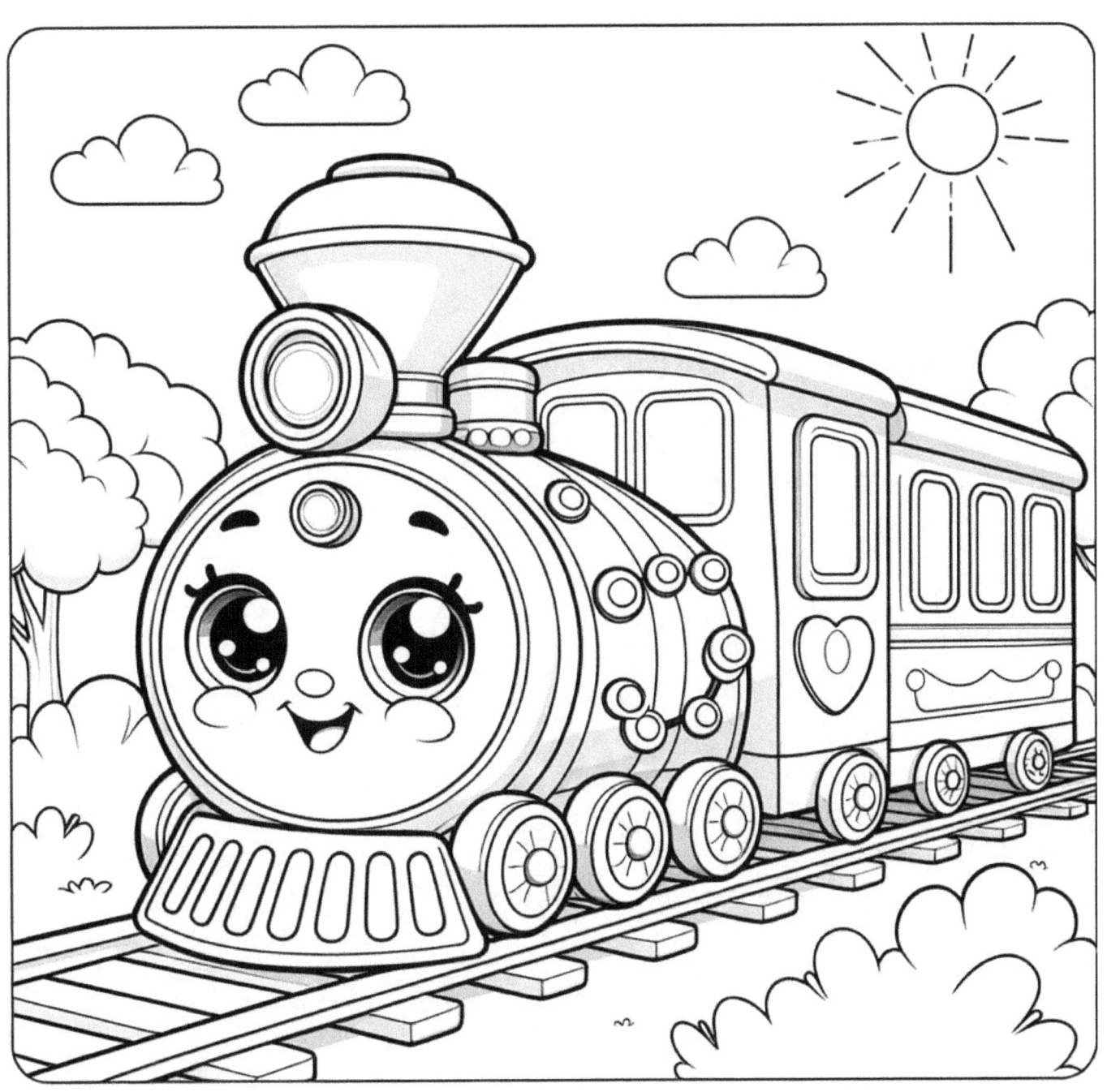

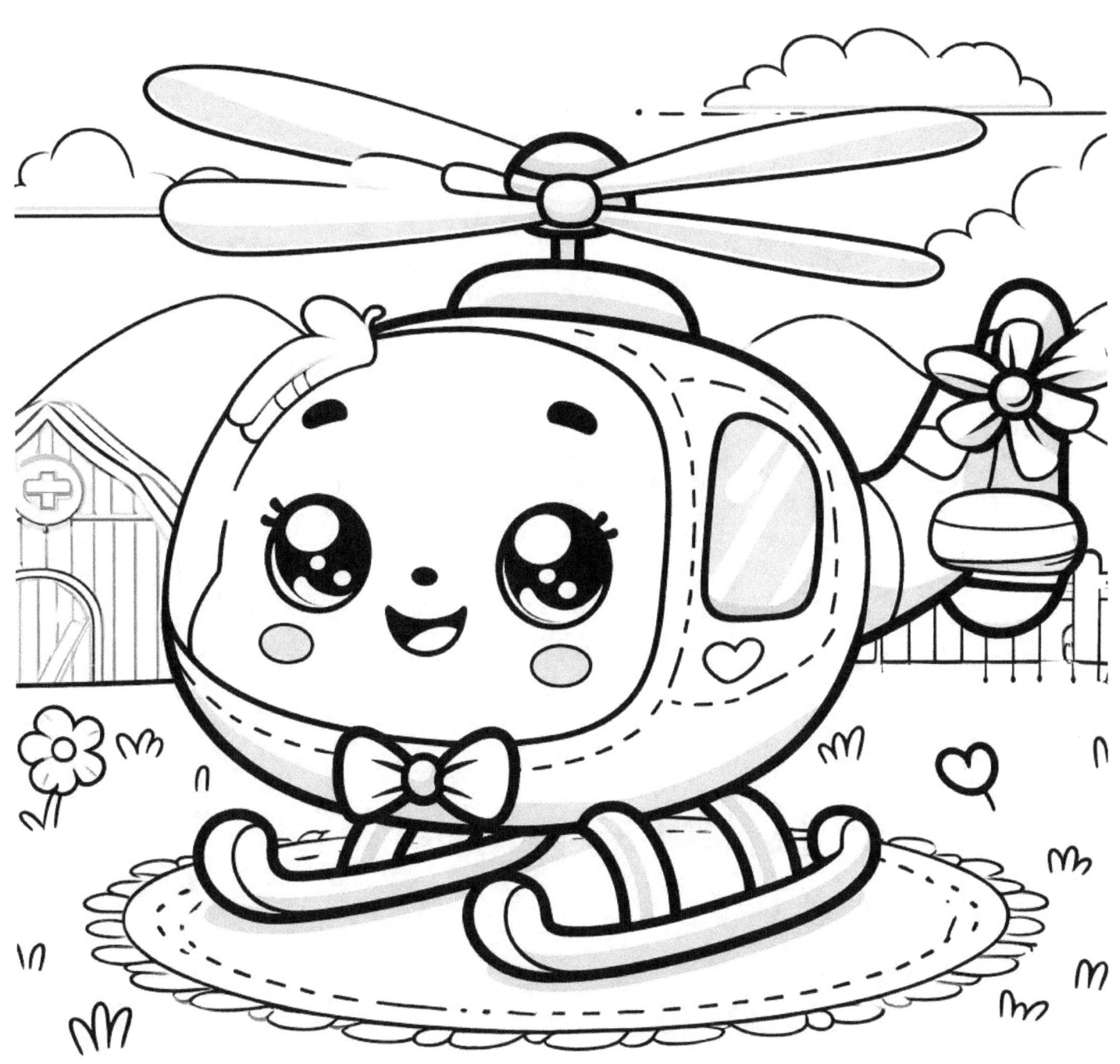

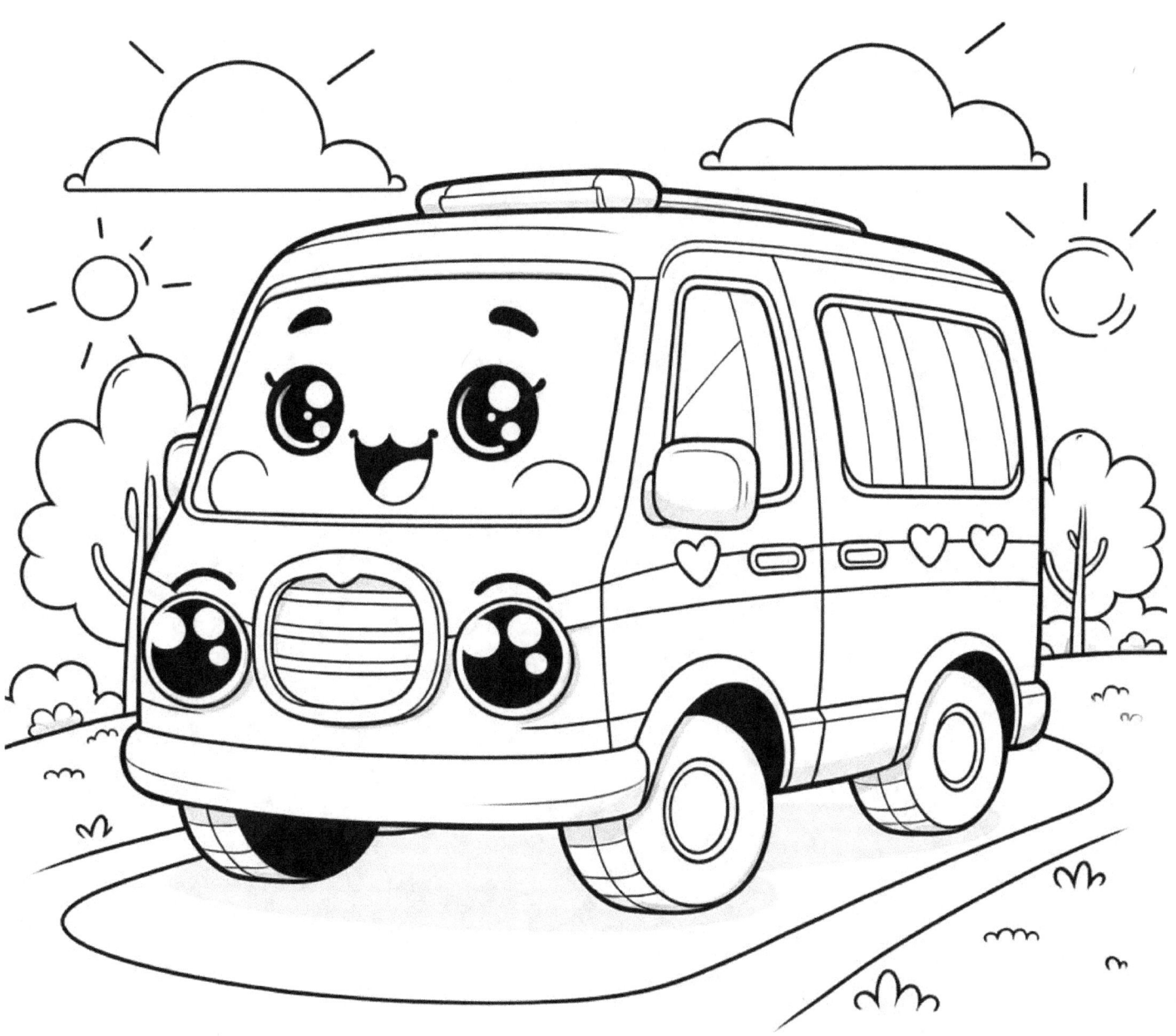

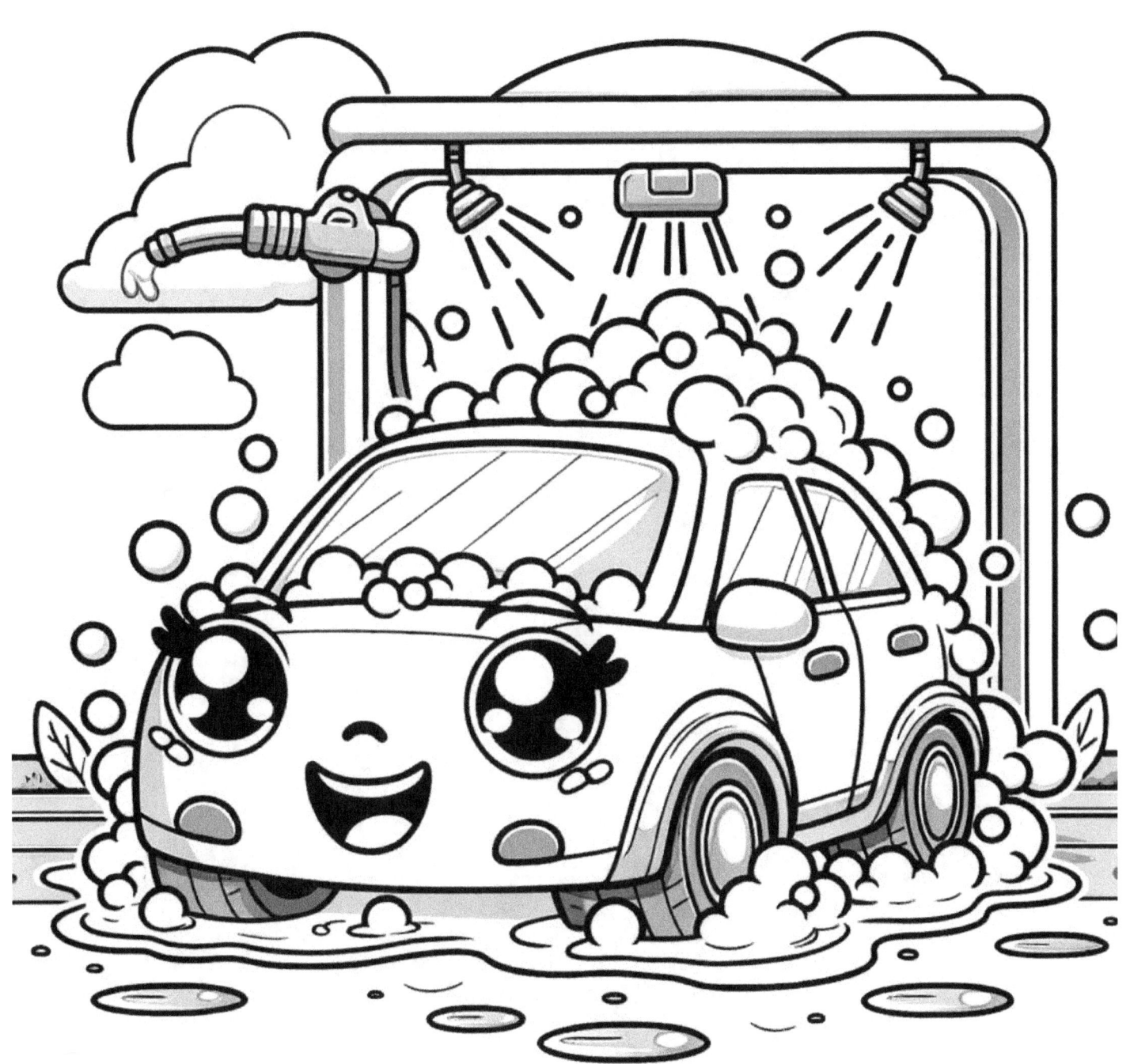

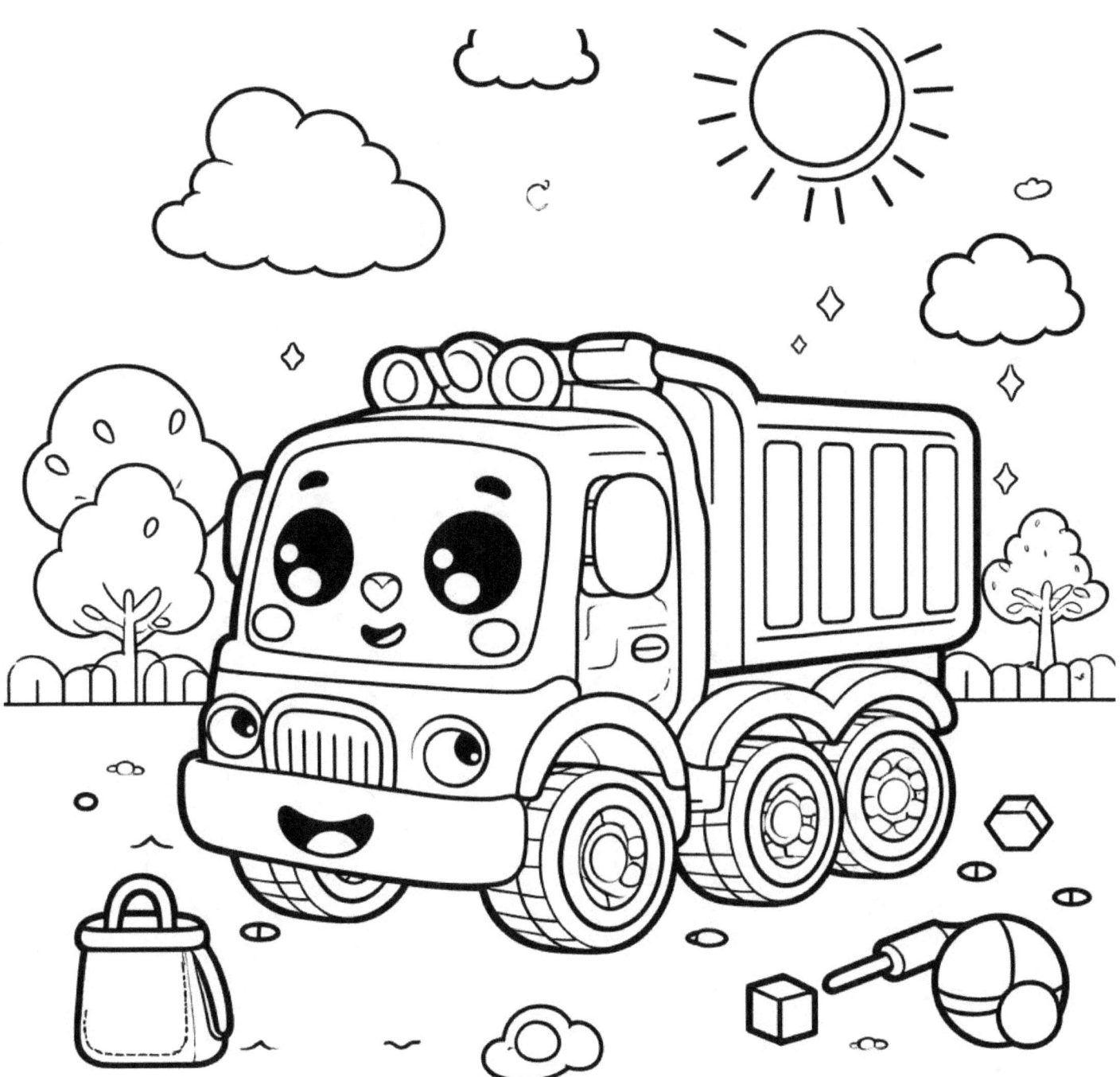

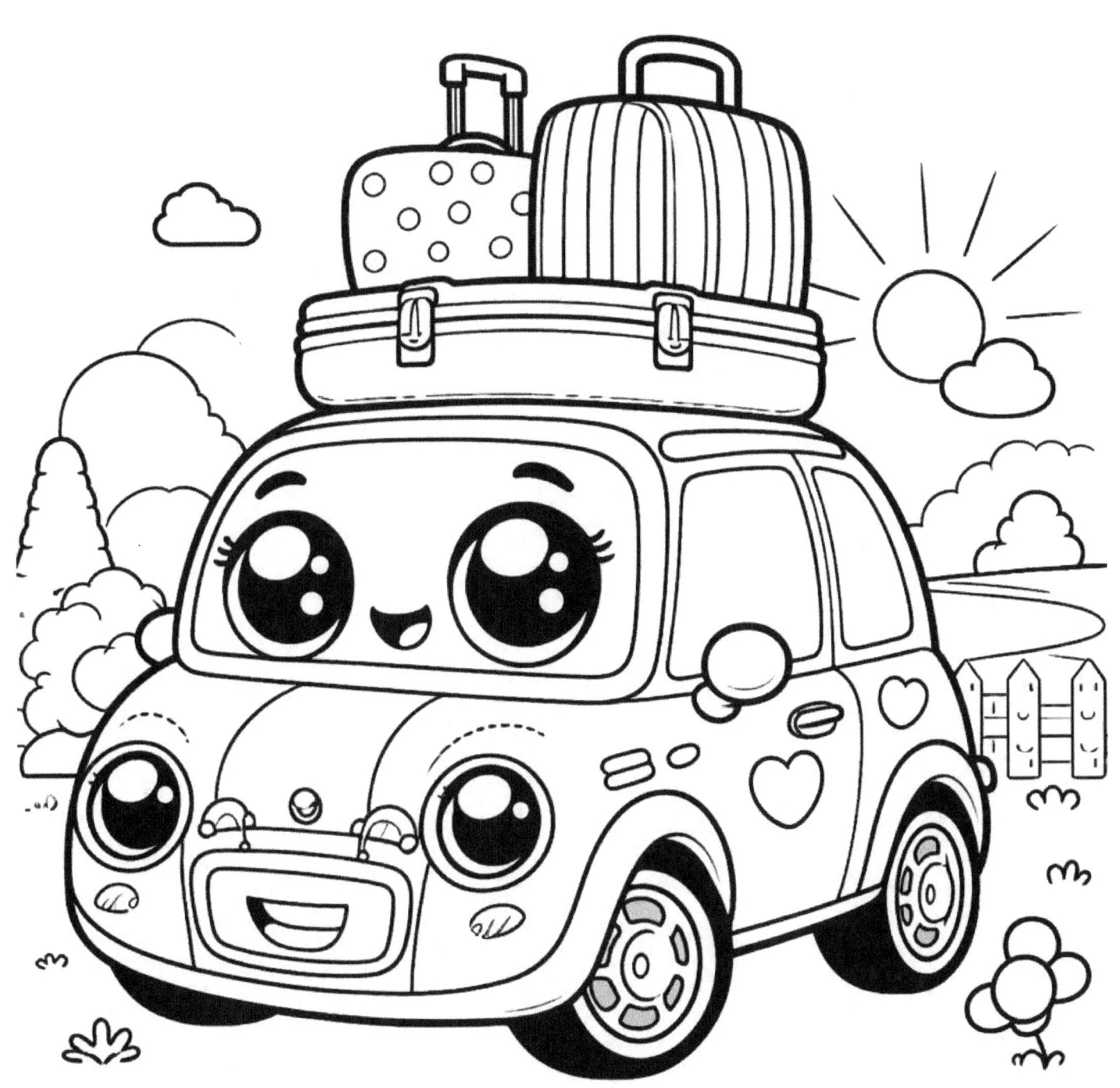

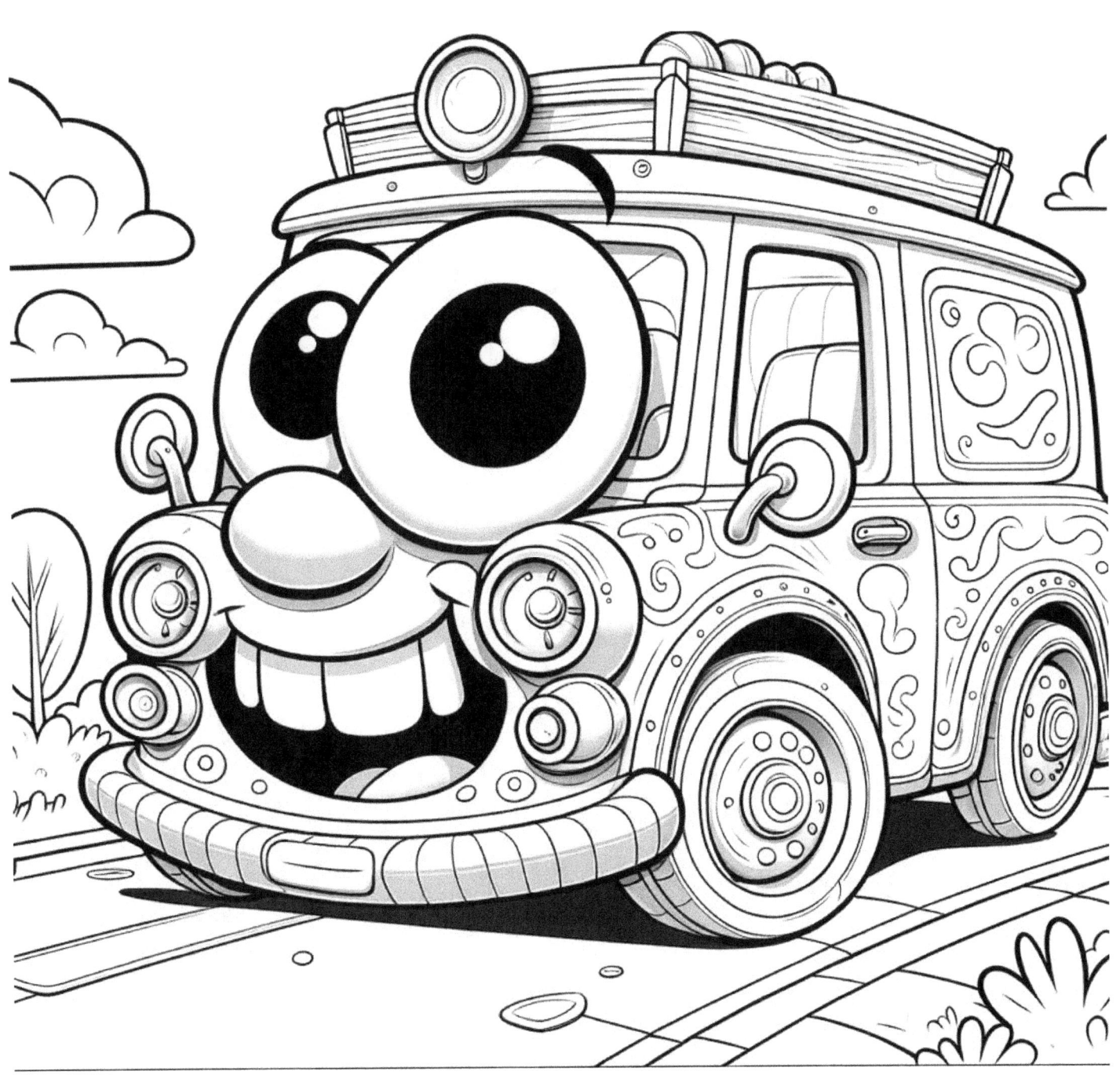

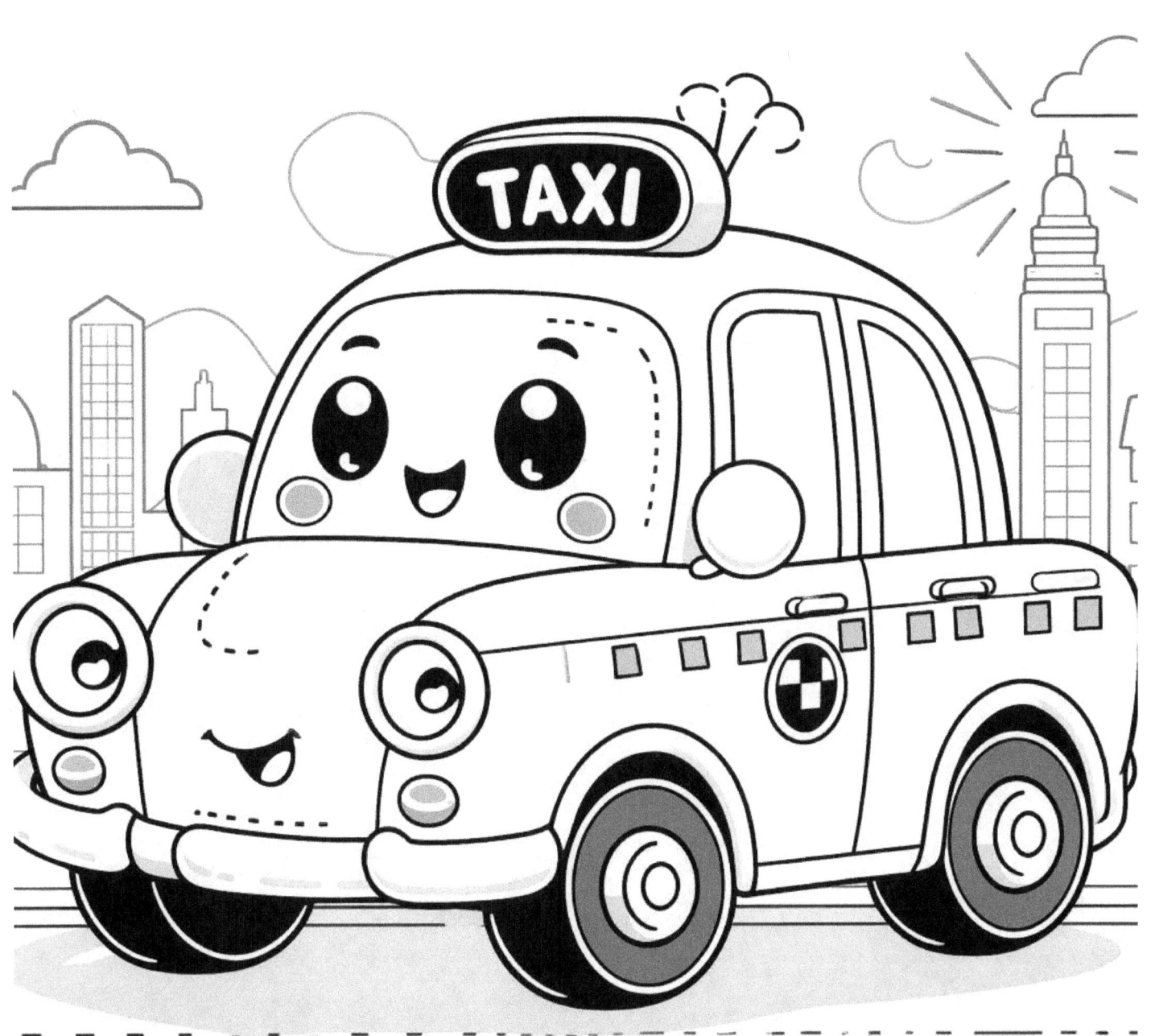

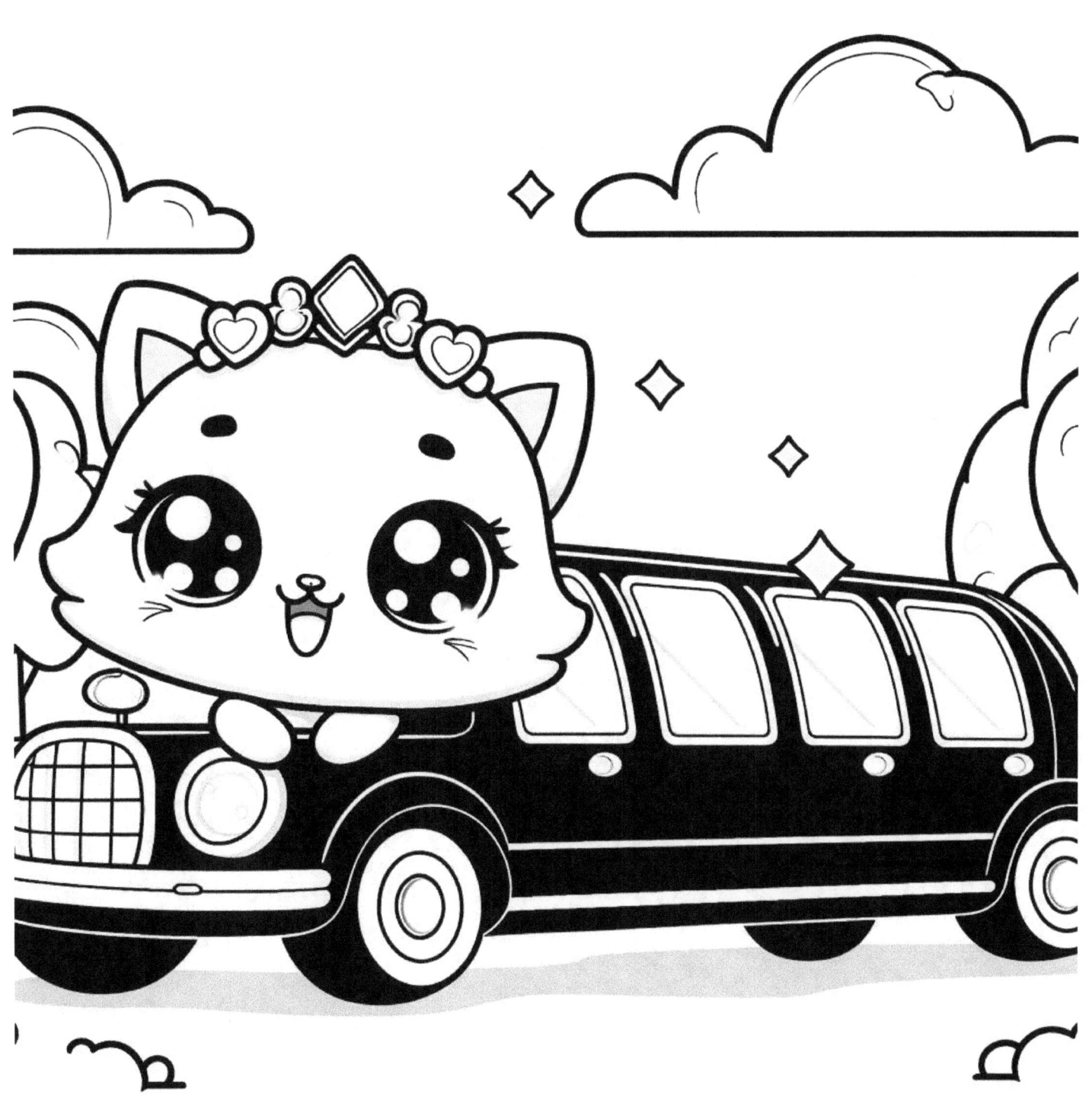

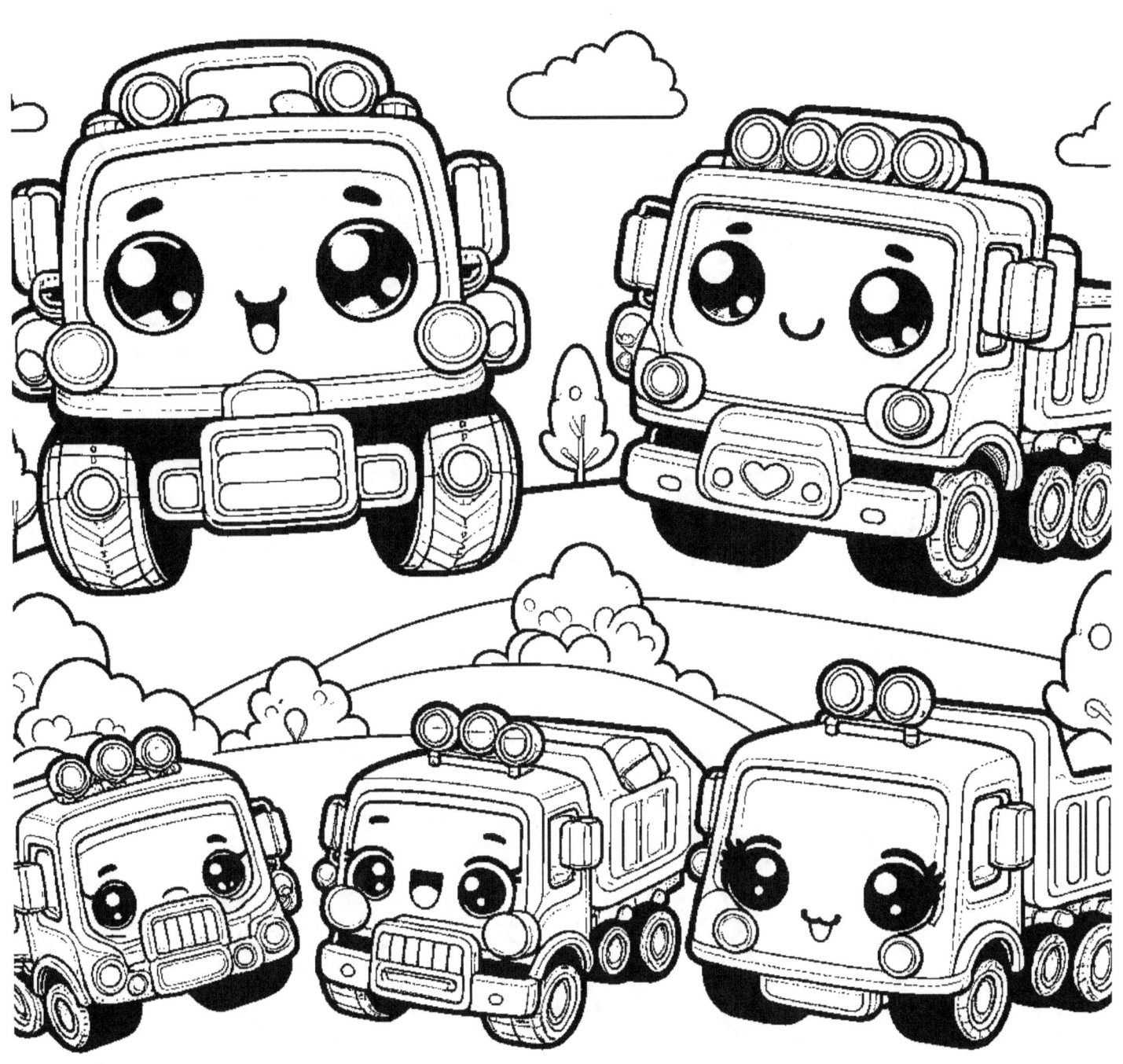

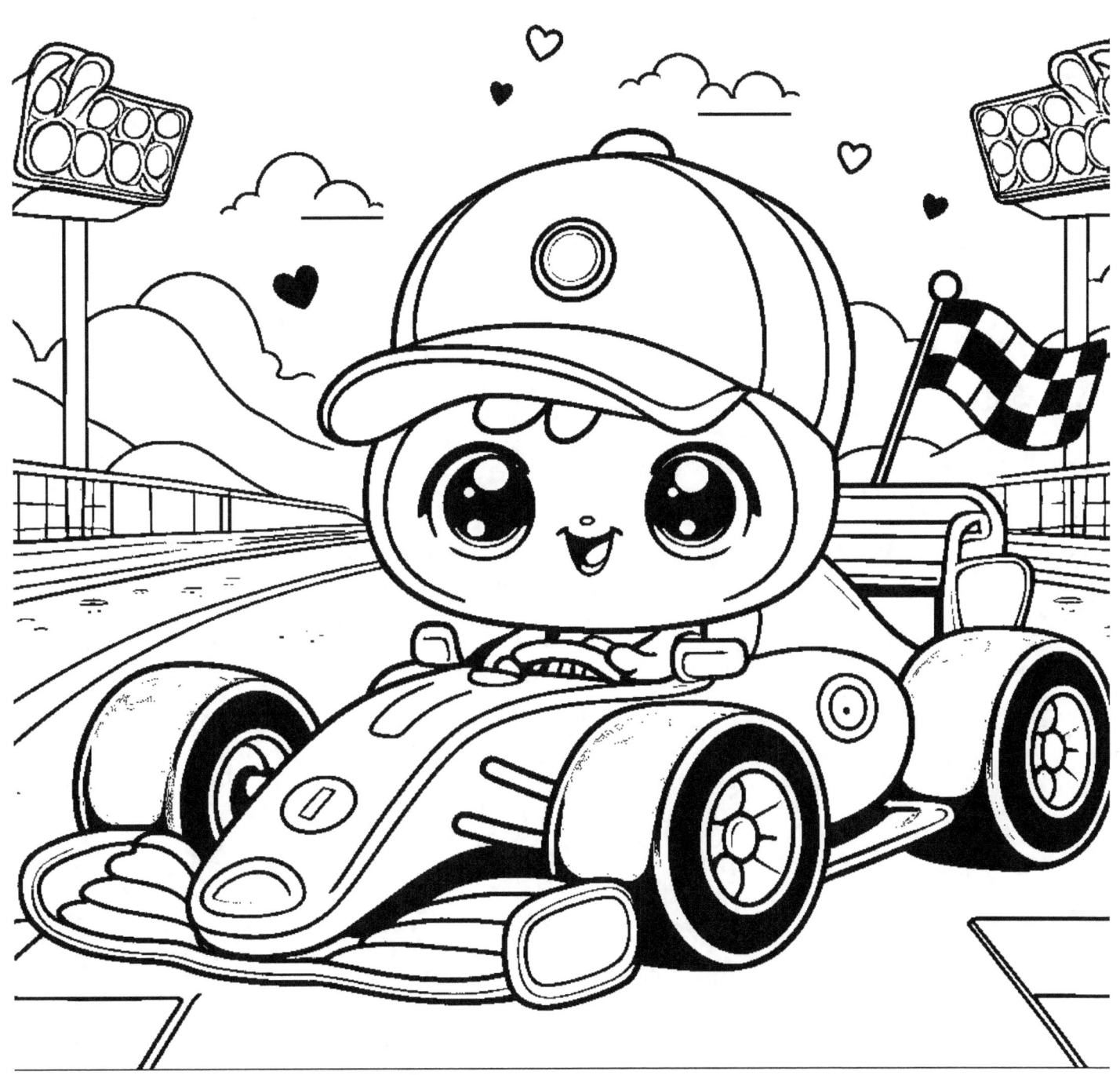

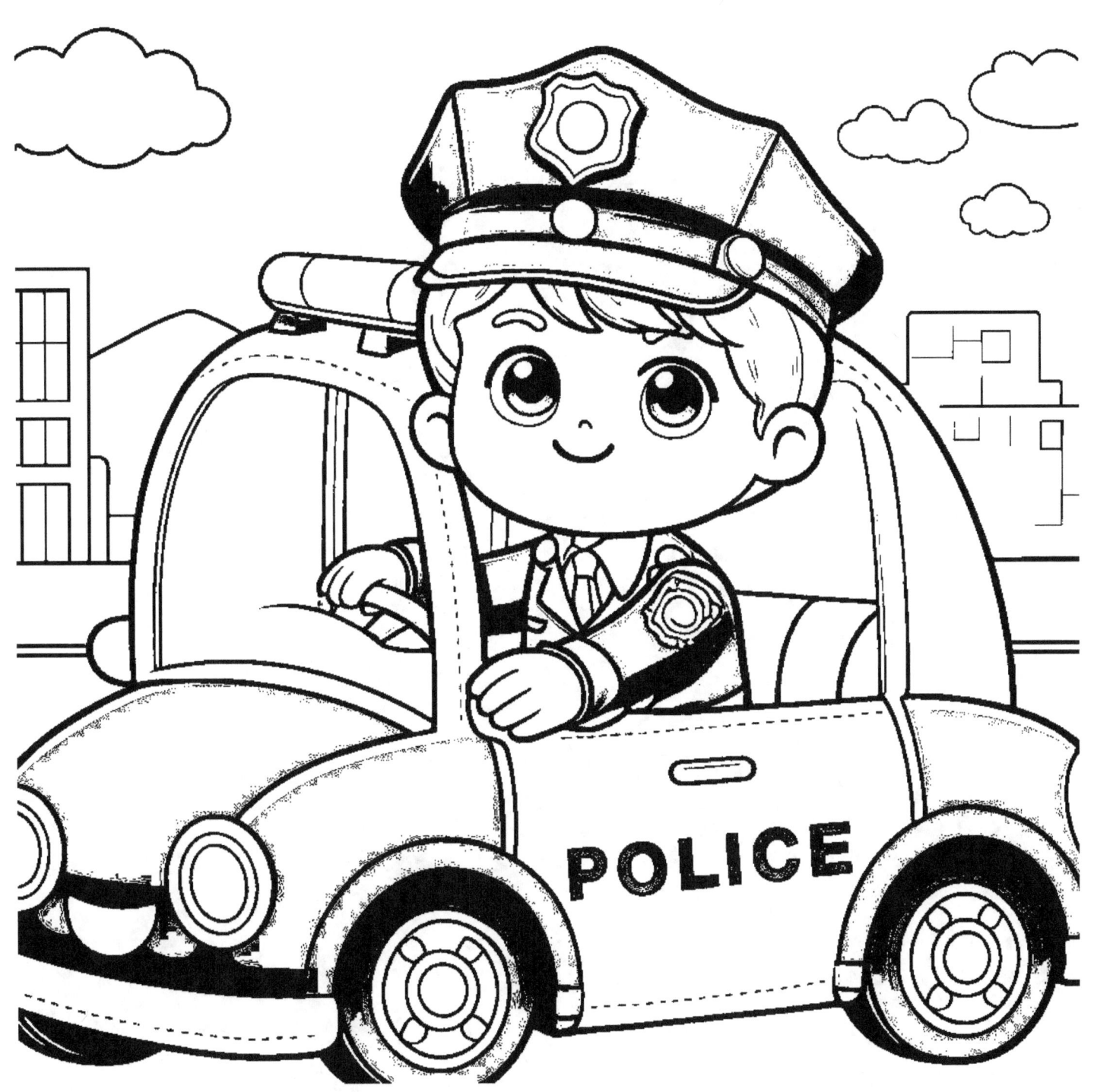

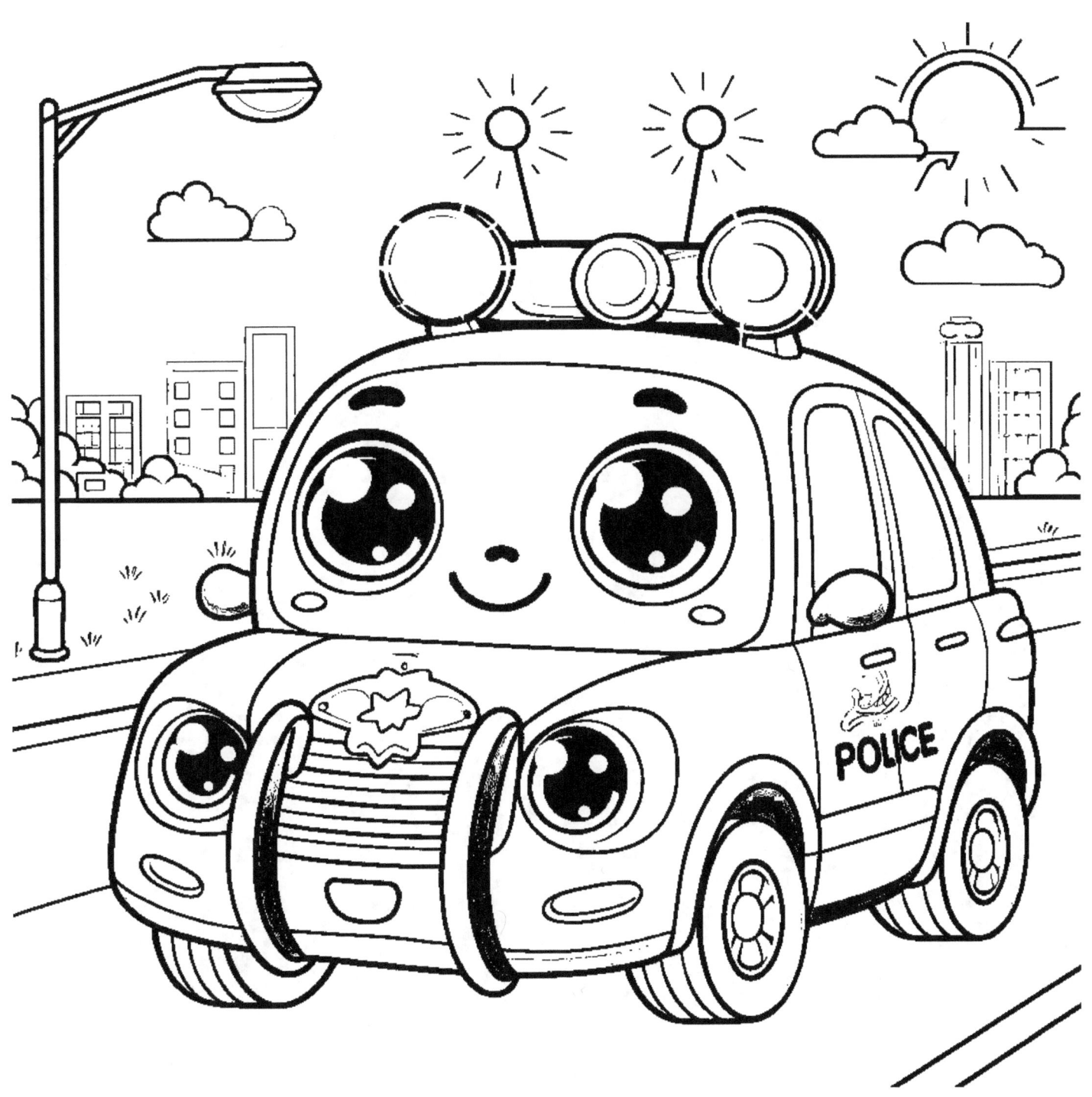

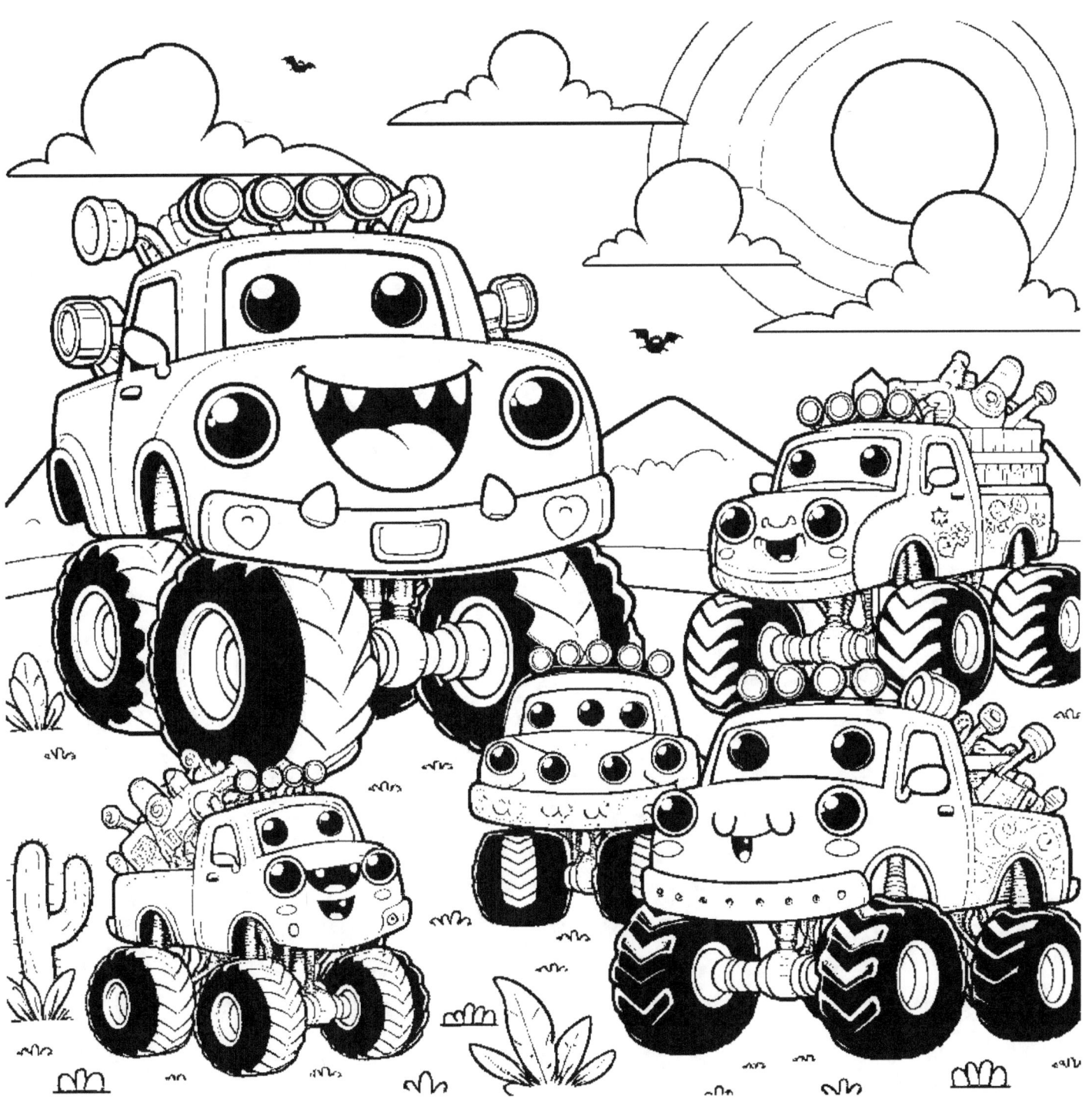

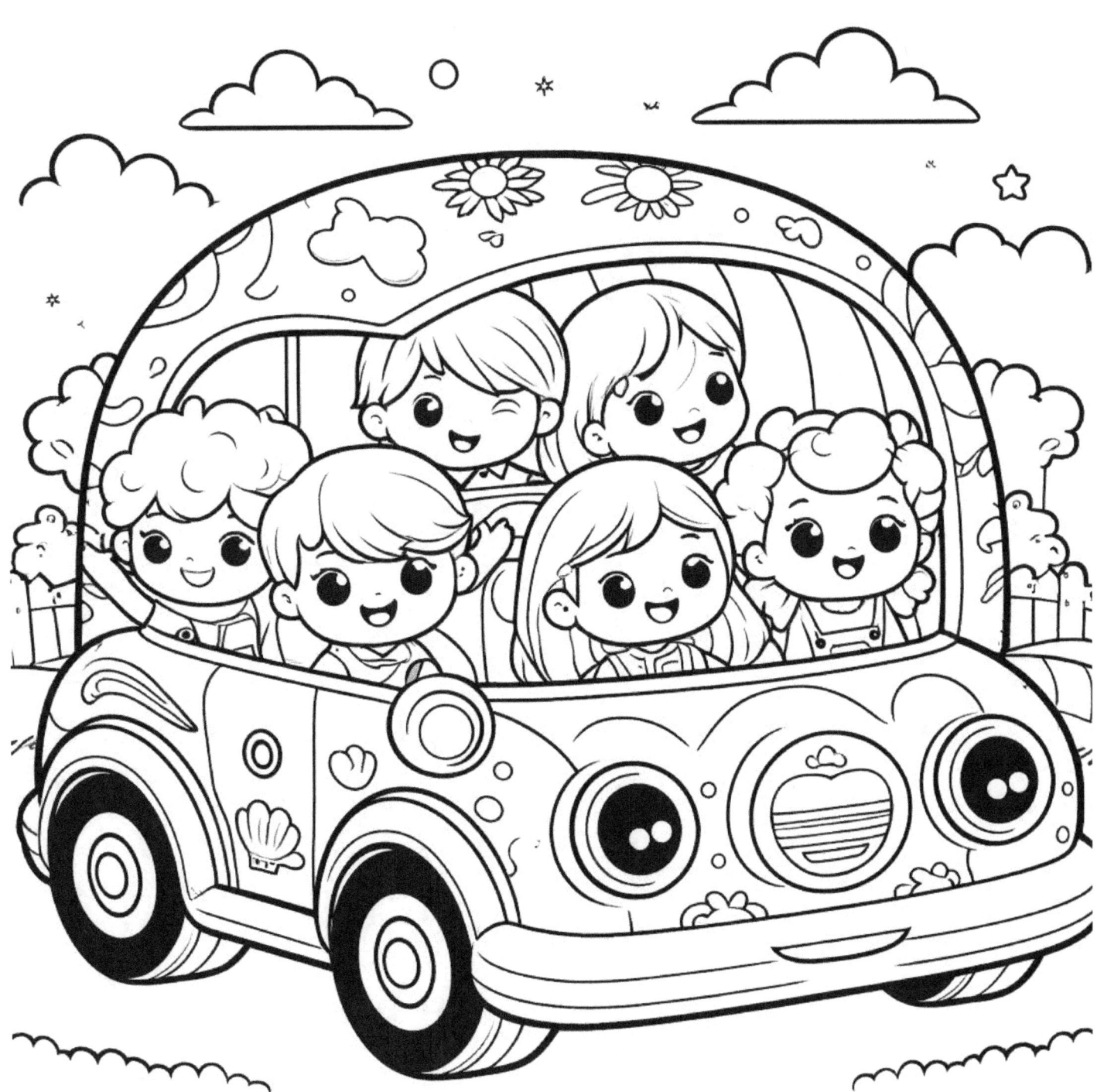

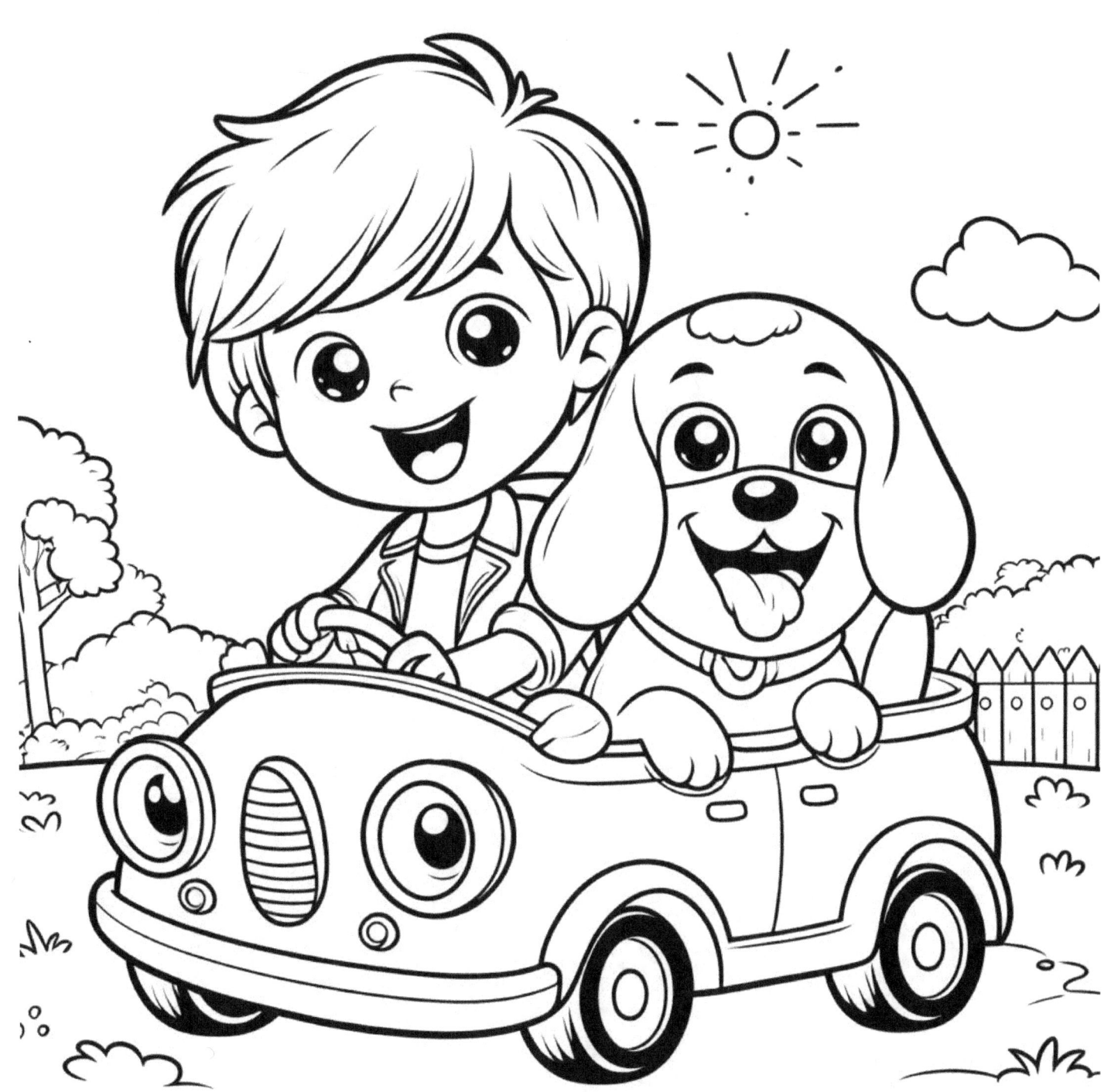

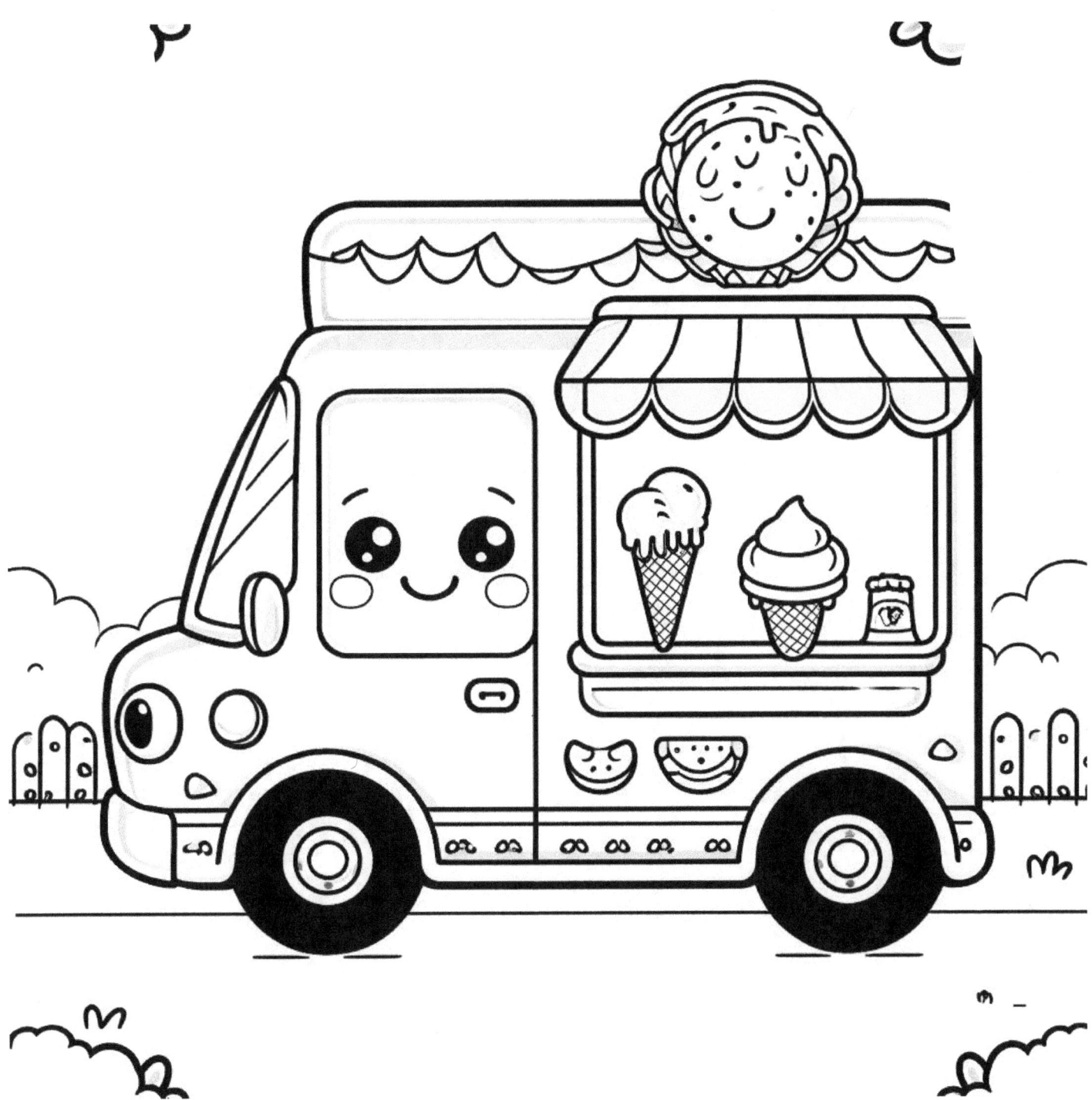

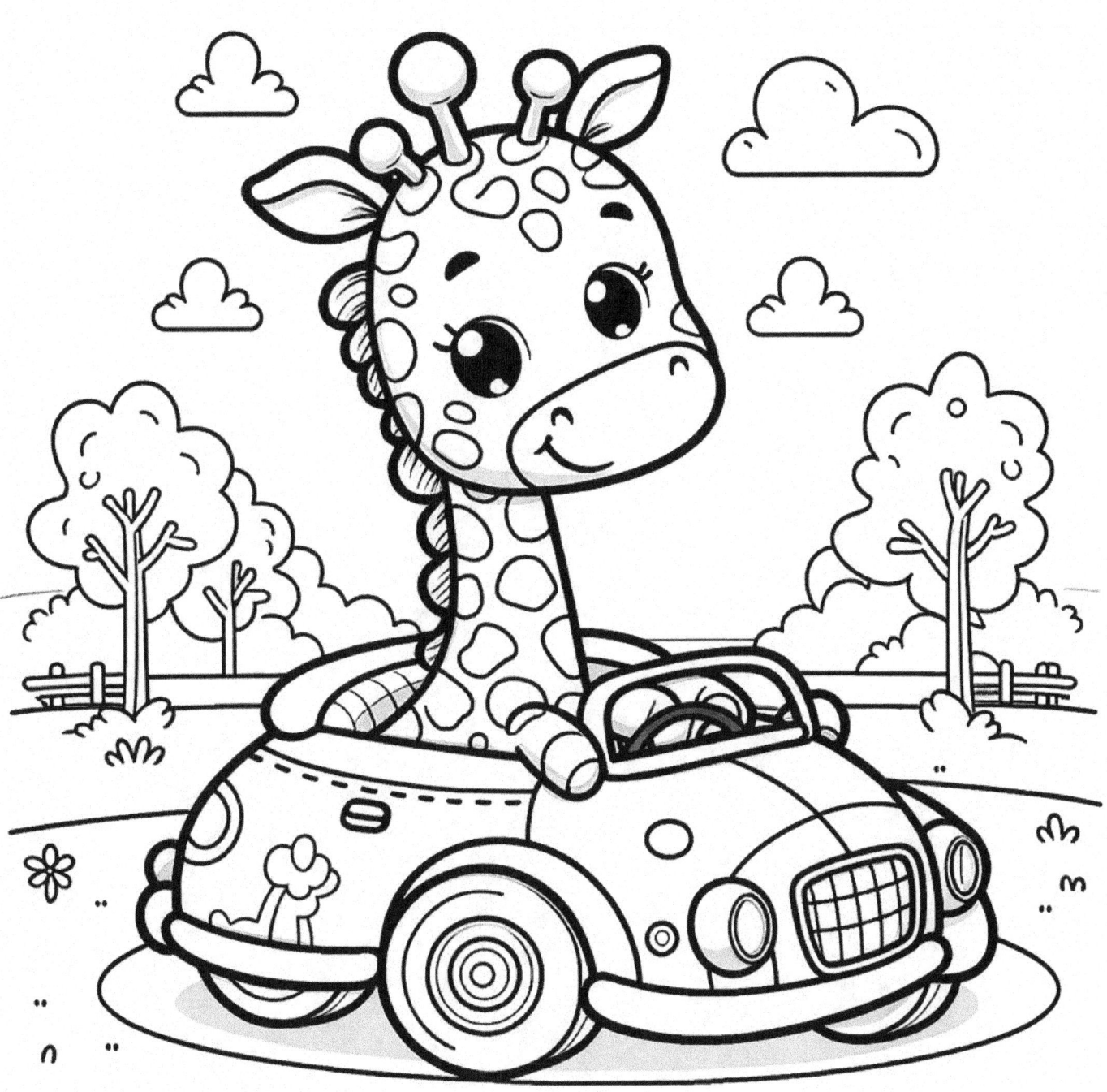

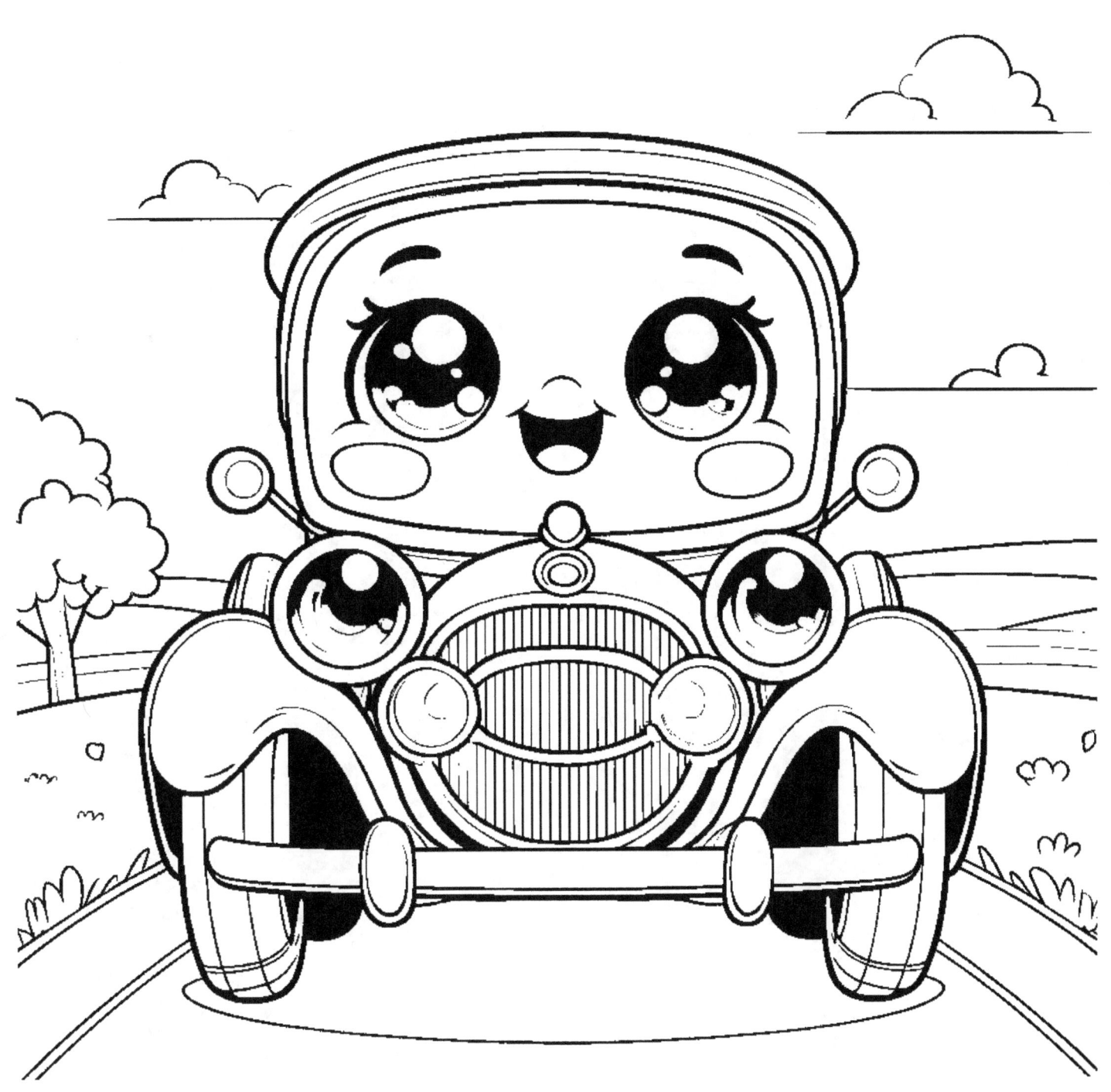

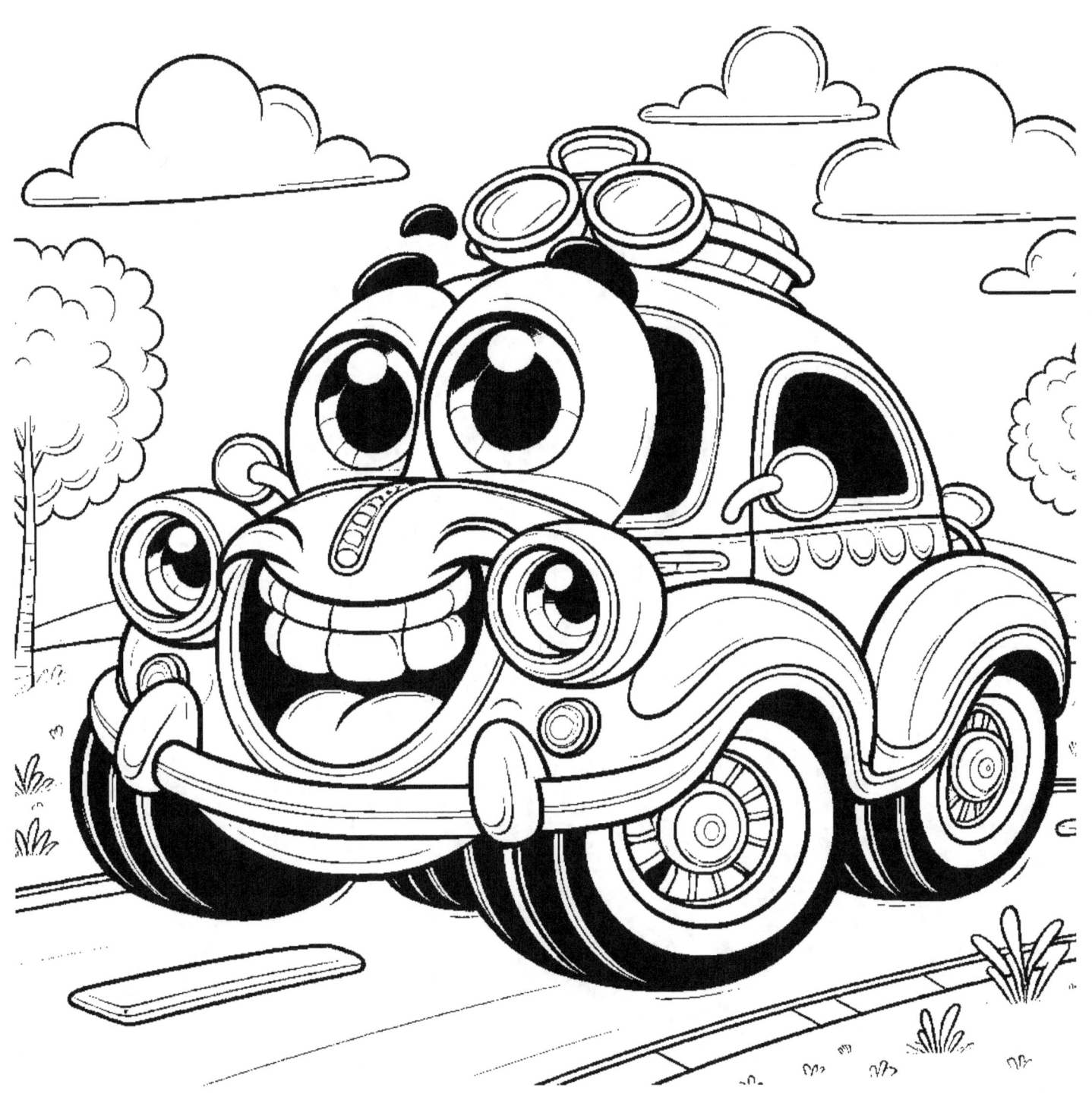

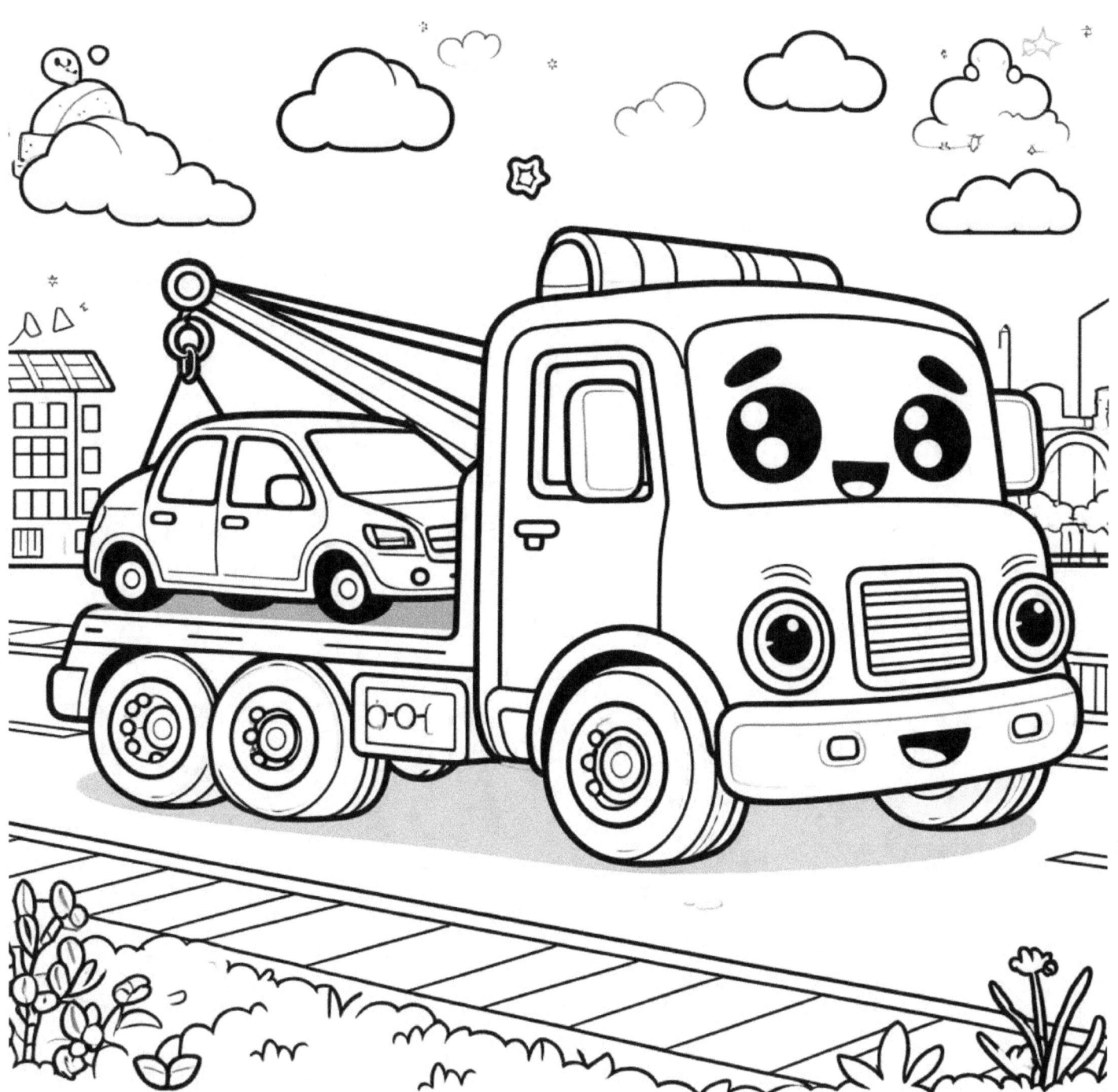

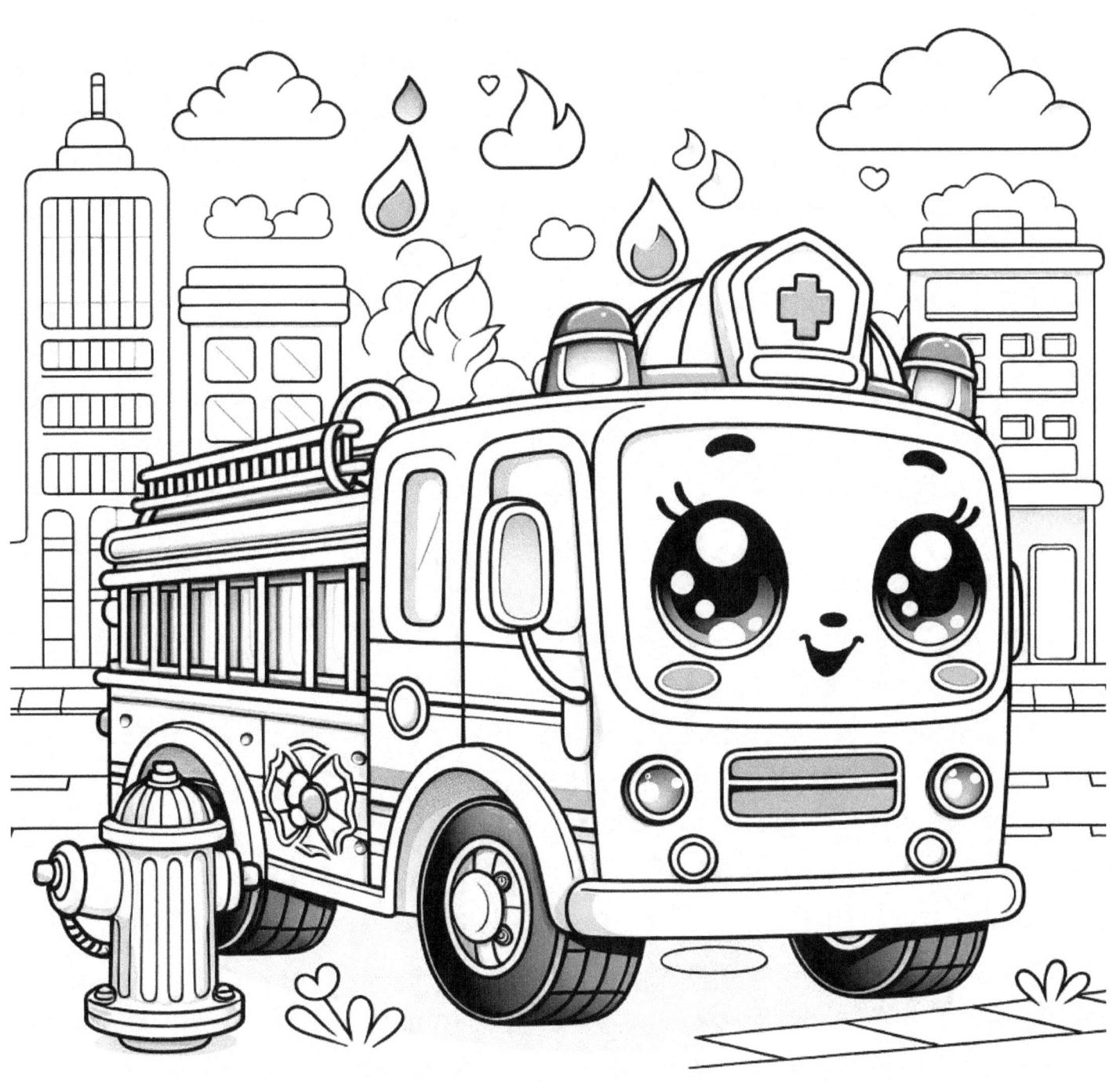

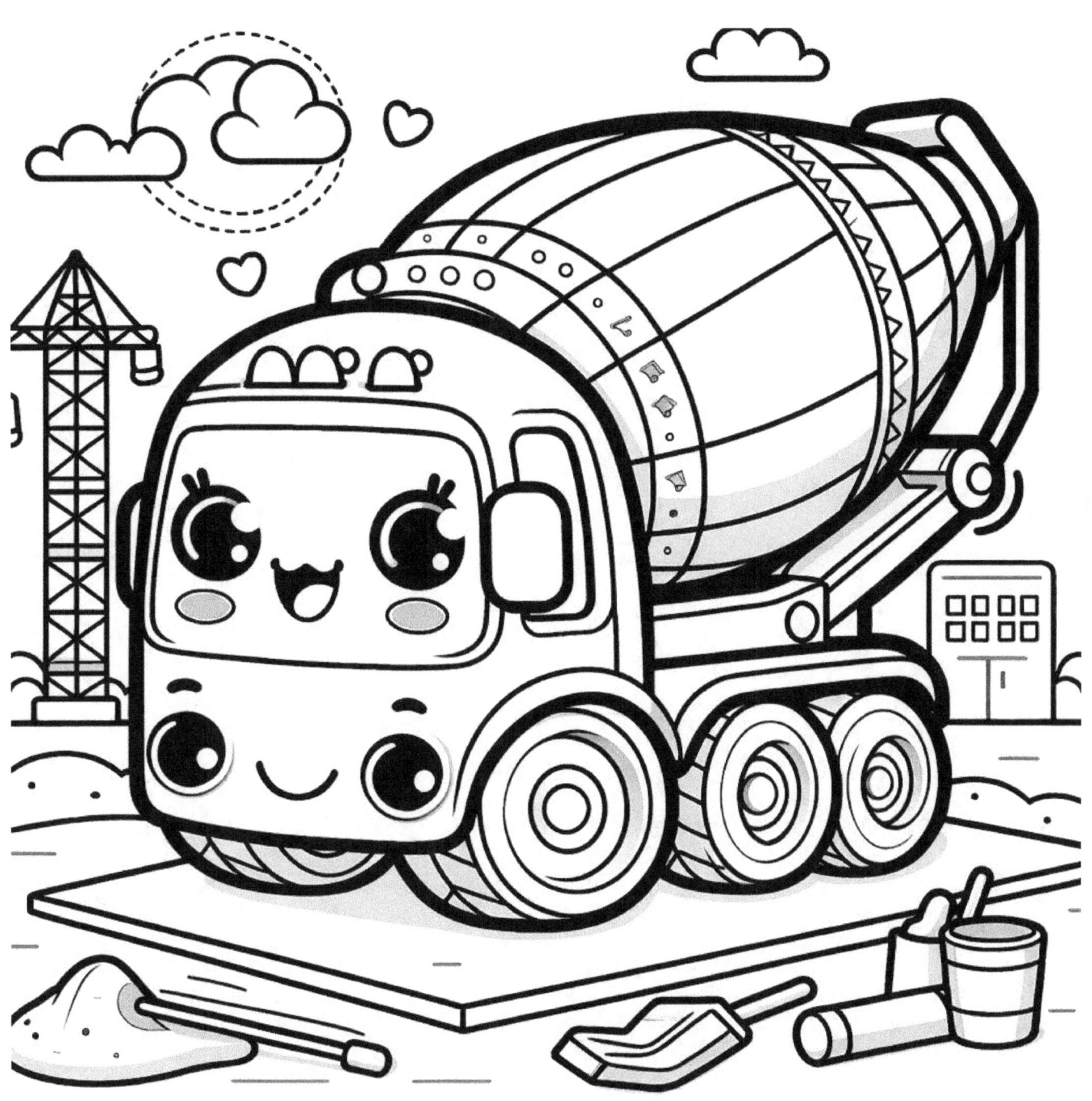

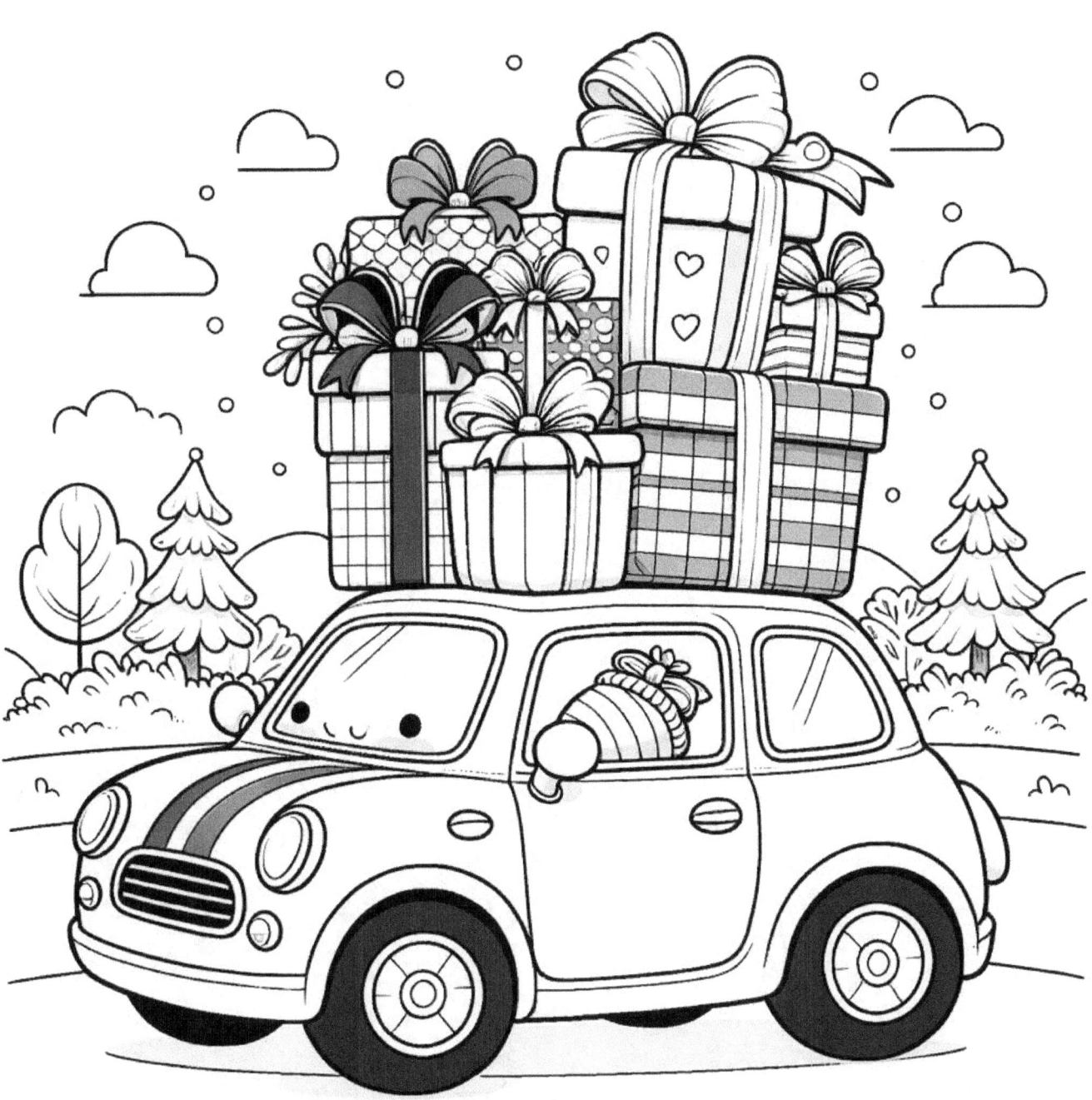

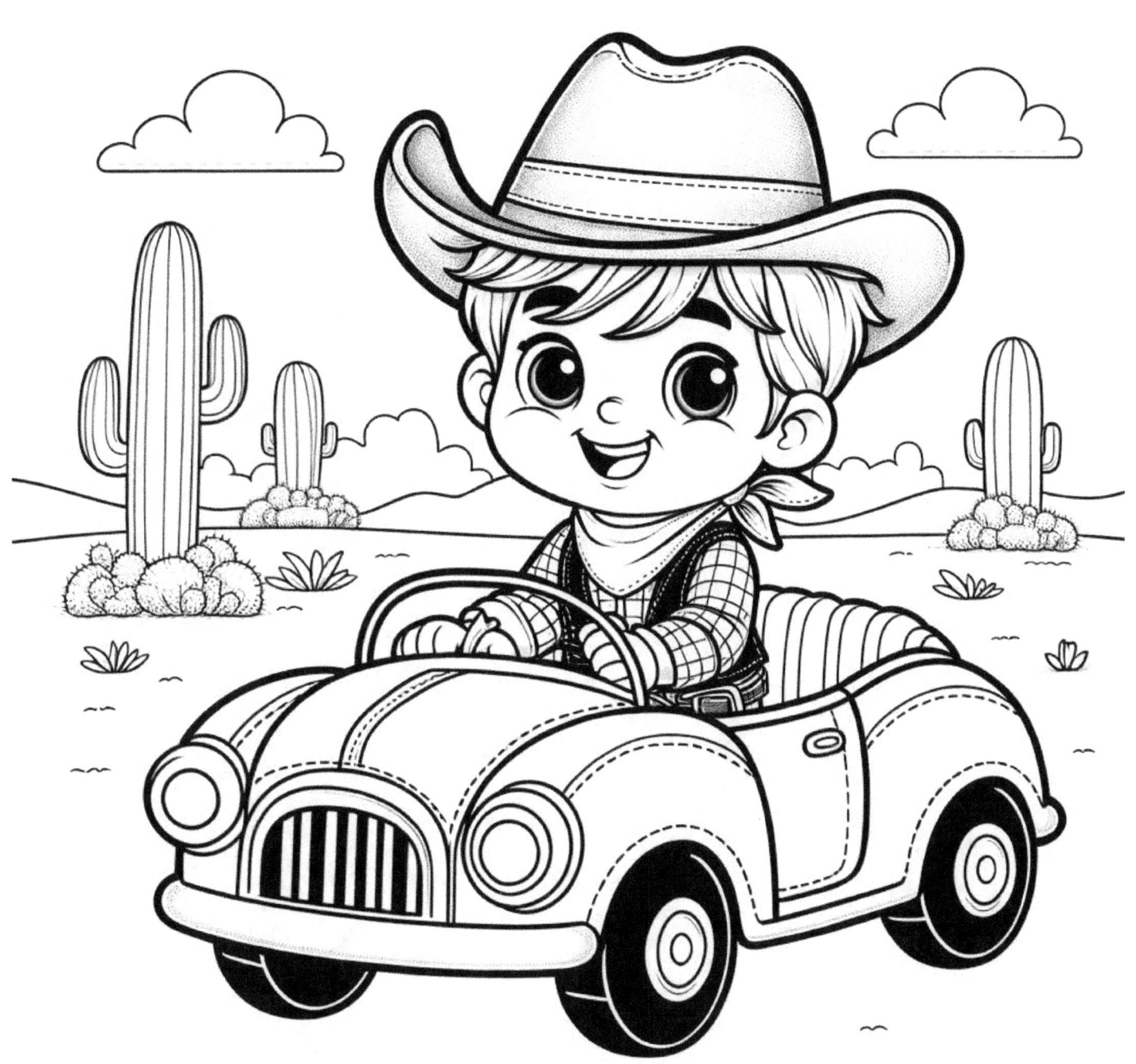

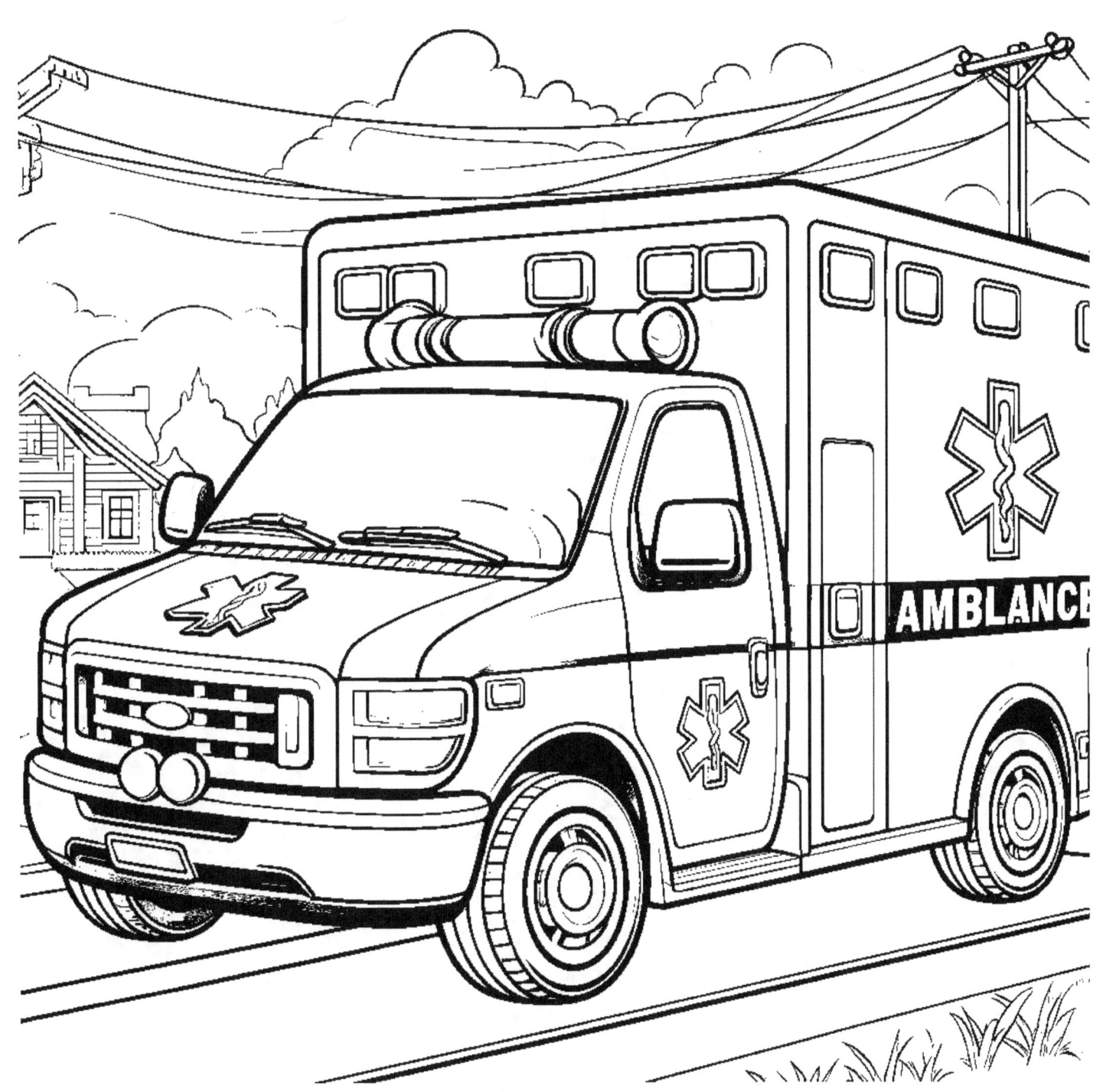

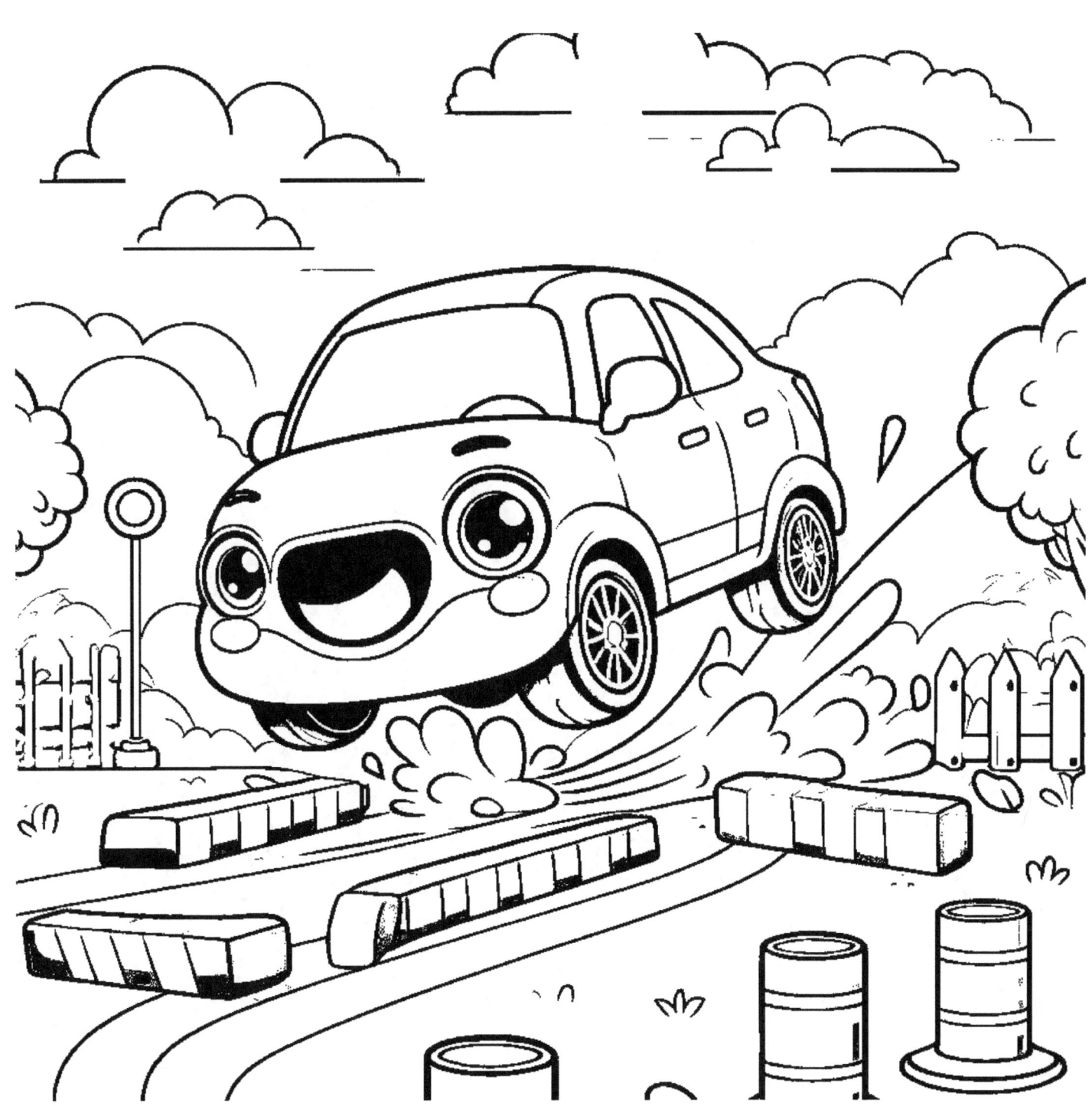

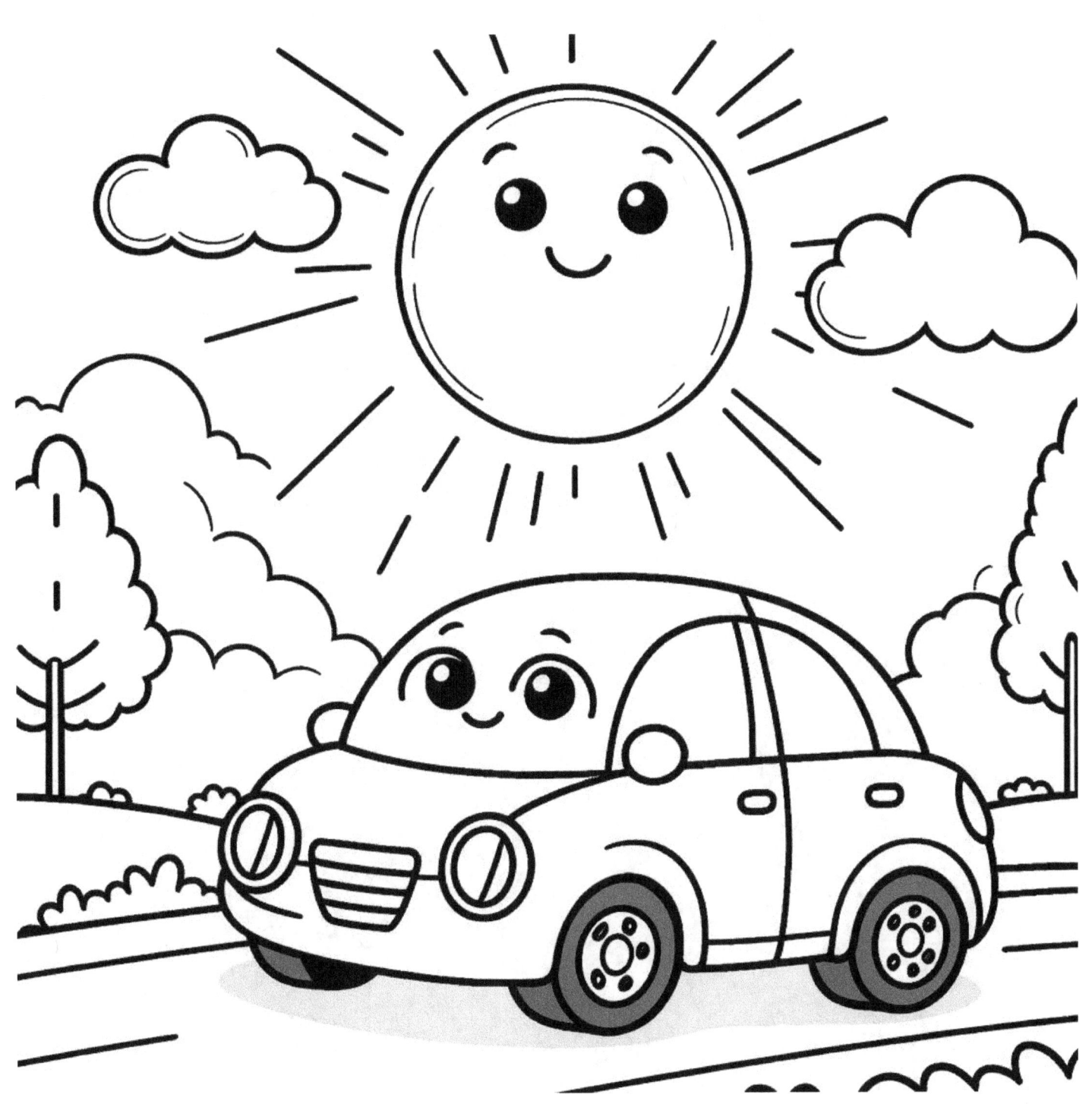

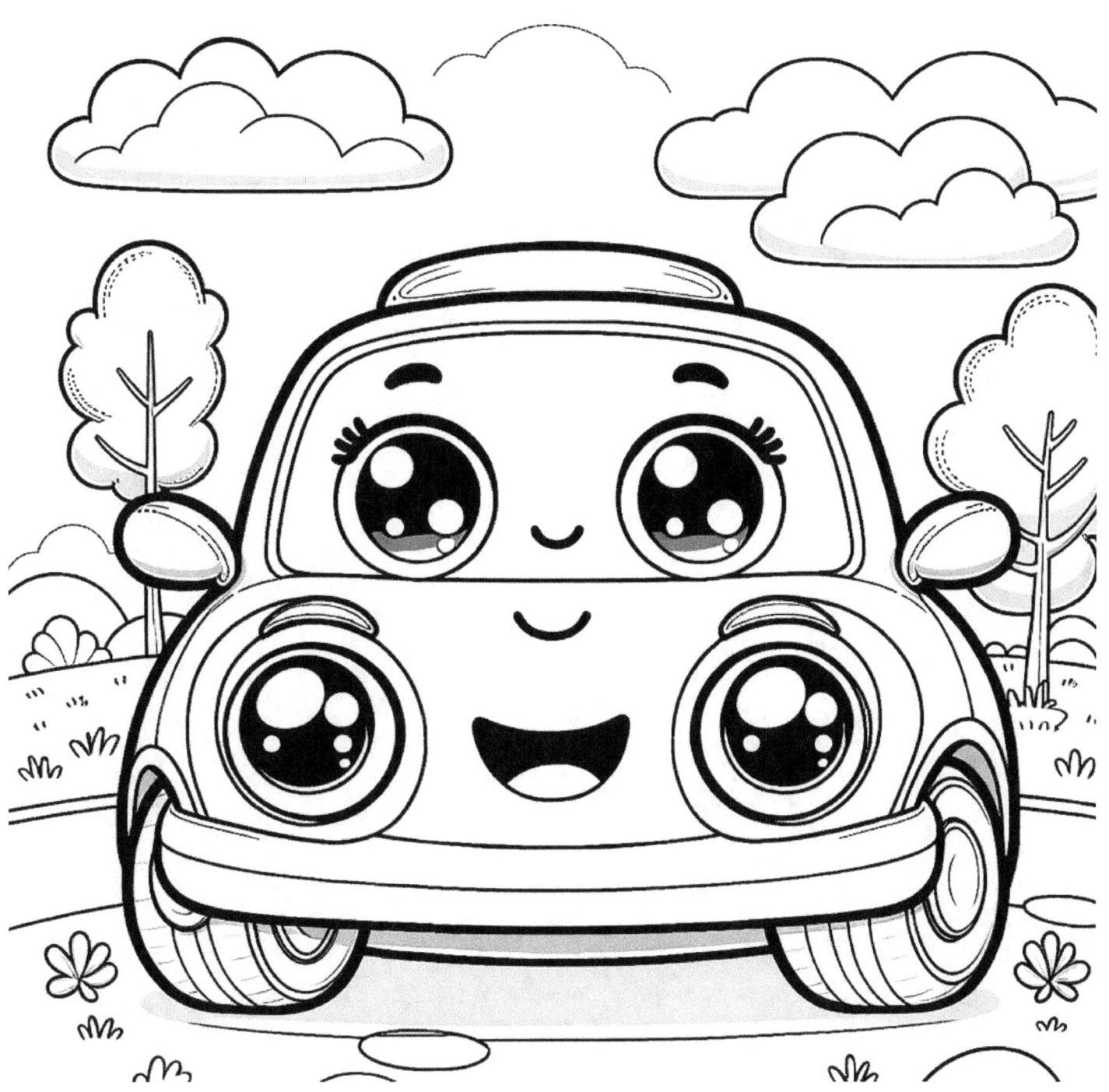

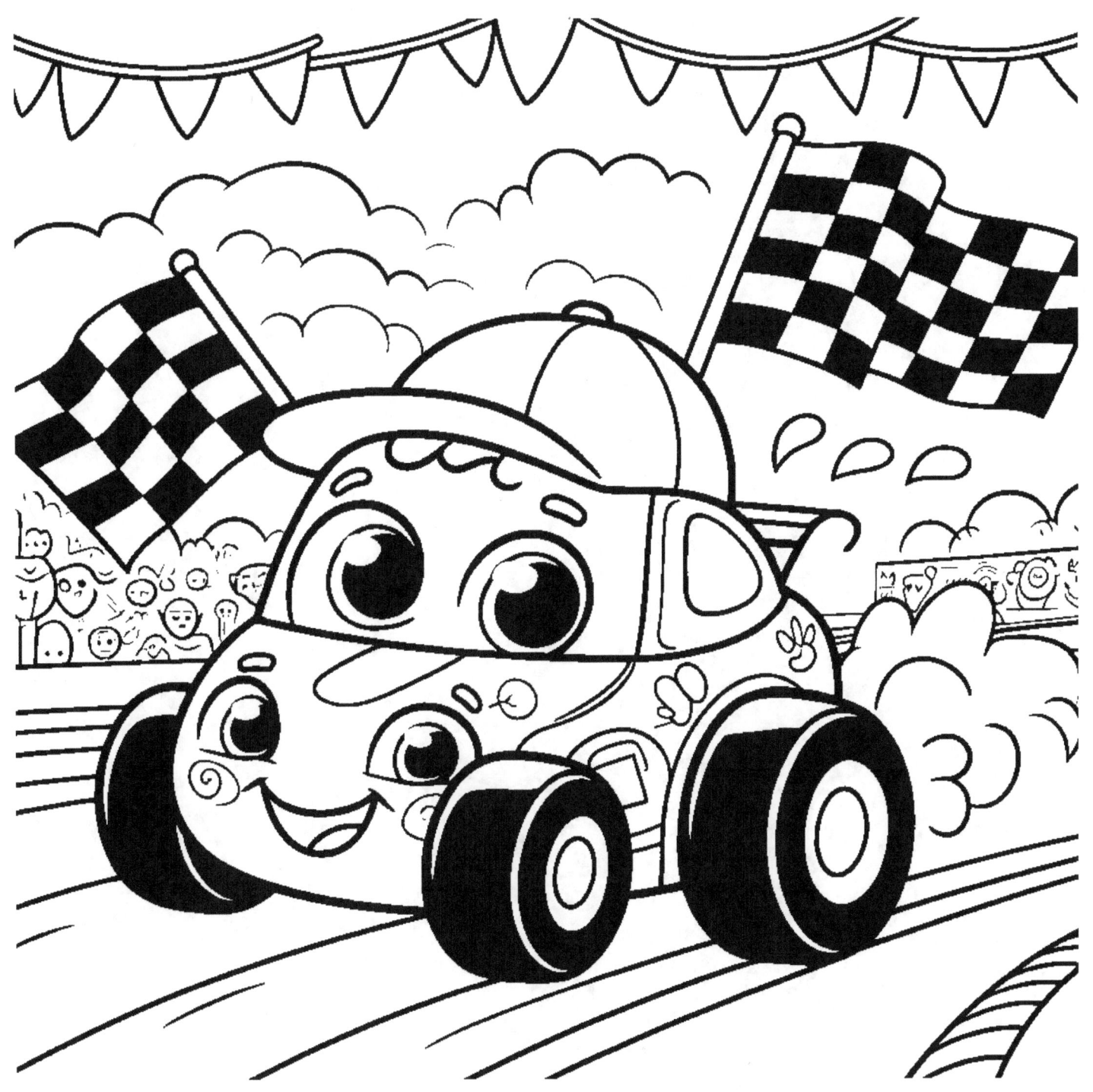

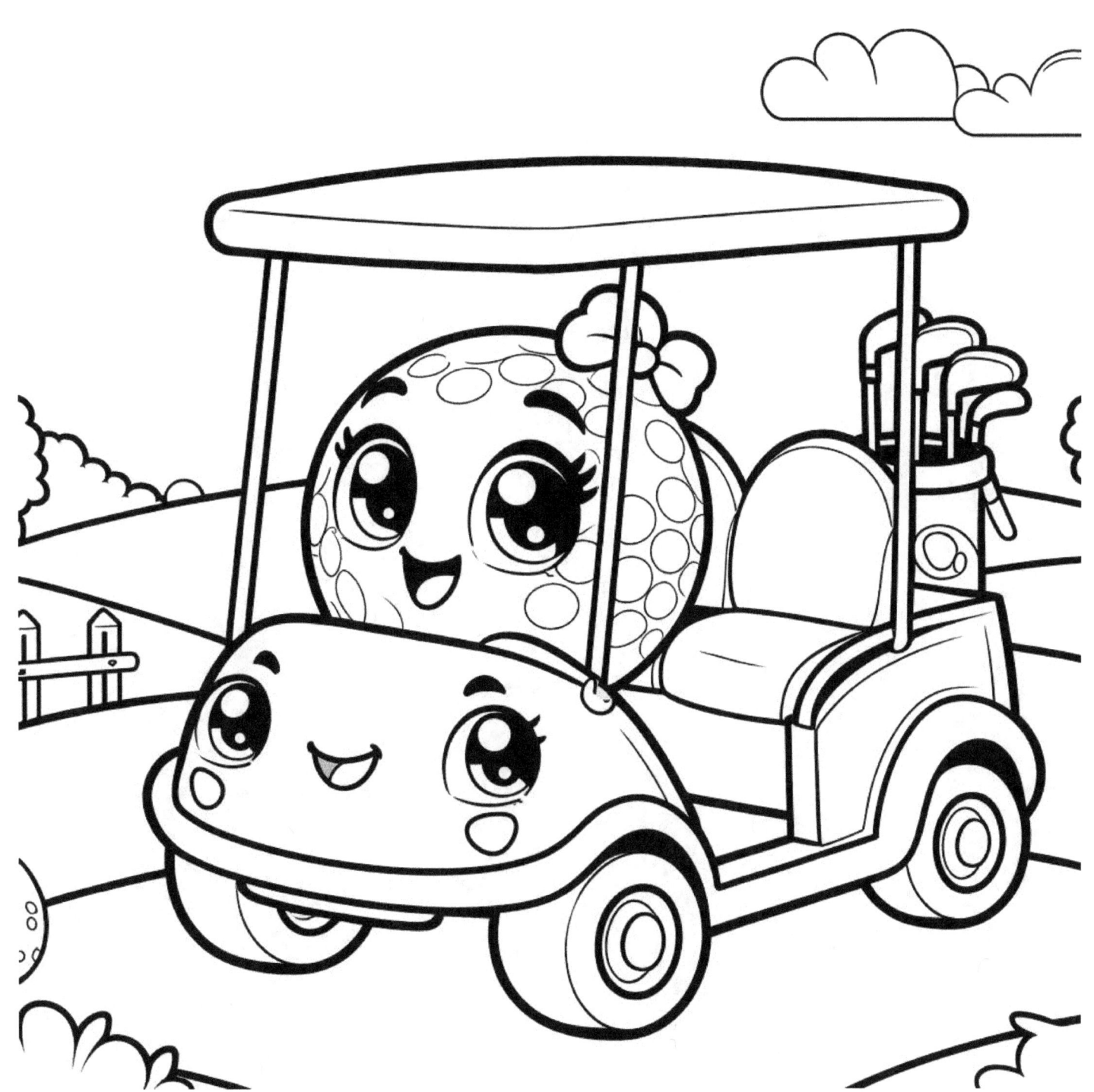

Conclusion

Thank you for buying this book, you can leave a review on Amazon saying what you liked or what you would like us to improve, until the next coloring adventure.

Pérez Arboleda